The Snoring of a Thousand Men

First edition published 3 September 2009, in commemoration of the 70th anniversary of the outbreak of the Second World War

First paperback edition (revised) 2011

ISBN – 13: 987-1456462253
ISBN – 10: 1456462253

Cover photo: digging for an Anderson shelter (see pp 23 and 56)

Published by Newcastle University of the Third Age (Newcastle U3A)
1 Pink Lane, Newcastle upon Tyne NE1 5DW UK
Printed by https://tsw.createspace.com   Text in Garamond

To those whose lives preserved our childhoods

Margaret Isobel Armstrong's Uncle Robert standing behind Prime Minister Winston Churchill and President Franklin D Roosevelt on HMS The Prince of Wales in 1941(see page 83-4). The ship was sunk later that year.

Note from the editor

Many of the contributors to this collection of memories were young children at home on Sunday, the 3rd of September, 1939, when Britain's Prime Minister announced that the country was at war with Germany, a war that was not to end till 1945.

Now, to their grandchildren, this is a distant era. British school projects have encouraged children to ask: 'What did you do in the war, Granny and Granddad?'. Such personal links with the past are fading, however. Everyday life during that world war, nevertheless, retains its lessons for today. The implications of climate change and the recent recession have reverberated memories of make-do-and-mend, managing-without, dislocation, anxiety – and resourcefulness, adapting to change, comradeship and making the best of things. For the grandparent generation brought up in wartime, there is something essentially valid and satisfying in this reversion to economising.

In commemoration of that momentous day over seventy years ago, and before these memories are lost, we asked senior members of Newcastle University of the Third Age (U3A) (see p 111) to record their personal experiences, emotions and anecdotes of the second World War. What follows is in their own words.

We have also added, to put the stories in their context, a list of the main landmarks of the wartime years, at home and on the front.

We gratefully acknowledge the time and energy that all the contributors have spent, particularly all the members of the Newcastle U3A Publications Team and, not least, Fay Weldon for her encouragement and kind words of approval.

Ruth Lesser

Contents

Foreword

Jay Weldon

I only have post-war tales to tell, but this collection of wartime memories from Newcastle U3A has set me off again. I found myself only yesterday going into elaborate detail about how my great-aunts in West Jesmond, Madge and Kitty Garbutt, taught me how to preserve an apple – to remove the core, slice paper-thin, thread the rounds on string and suspend in a jam jar of sulphur fumes, bake overnight - and at the end of all that work one single dried, preserved apple to last the winter through. The triumph of it! I recalled the high coiled spring beds, and the damp cosy steaminess of unaired stiff white linen sheets, and the ice flowers on the inside of the bedroom windows, and how, fresh off the boat from New Zealand in 1946, aged 15, I managed to get their entire week's butter ration on to one slice of National wheatmeal bread, toasted. I'm still ashamed – and still eat far more butter than I should. It's as if I will never get enough, and it's the same, I find, for many women of my age. We both love the frugality of those years, and can never quite deal properly with plenty.

What I didn't have to live with was what all the other contributors to this book did - the sense of fear as death rained from the skies, in the form of bombs and bullets, as in David Woodroff's *Bombers over the Thames*. There he is, an innocent lad cycling down a country lane with friends when a German bomber bursts through the mists and over and past them, only for the rear gunner to let off a burst of machine gunfire at them. At children! It seems unthinkable now – but that's how we were, on both sides. The excitement and danger of war sends men mad, and we'd better remember it. Those rear gunners seldom lived. They too were young, and frightened, and desperate.

In Dorothy Fawthrop's lovely piece *Shared beds and shared schools* she and her mother were so scared they just clung together, as if paralysed, when the bombs approached, when they should have been running for the stairs. It's frightening just to think of it; she was lucky – but then all the contributors to this book were blessed by luck. Like David Woodroff they were the ones who lived to tell the tale. And survivor guilt takes many forms – here's Marguerite Rook in her piece *A bomb in our garden* still feeling guilty about having prayed for Hitler to come and bomb the school so she wouldn't have to go to lessons – and the school was bombed, but lessons just carried on under another roof. So it goes.

Like Dorothy, I too remember knitting for the troops. I was at a convent school in Christchurch, New Zealand. We'd sit at our desks and knit balaclavas and sing as we worked –

'Knitting, knitting, knitting,
With a prayer in every row,
That the ones we love
By God above,
Will be guarded as they go.'

I was rather sorry for the troops. The wool was stringy and hard and such a dull khaki colour and the balaclavas we knitted sometimes looked quite peculiar, but we did our best. It was the war effort, after all.

Peter Jones' *VJ Day (and what to do with a surplus bomber)* put me in mind of another incident. We may not have had bombs in New Zealand but we were certainly frightened, and there were air-raid drills. It was 1942. All the young men had gone off to war: it was a nation of women and children. The Japanese were on course to invade New Zealand after their victory in Bataan. I asked my mother why she was teaching me and my sister to say 'yes certainly' in Japanese, 'kan-ar-a-zu' - and she

10

said darkly it was because the neighbours were saying if the Japanese came we girls had to be killed to save us from their vile clutches, but she thought this was the better option.... The Japanese never came, the Americans having turned up with a week to spare – and a couple of years later Japanese mothers were saying the same thing, having the same fears, about the Americans.

But all the tales brought back such vivid memories: the make-do-and-mend enthusiasm – my gran's underwear made out of parachute silk (parachutes never lay long in the fields: the village girls would have them in no time); pencil lines up the back of your legs - second best to non-existent silk stockings – the Americans brought nylons with them, miraculously thin and glassy; vegetables growing where once roses did; whale meat for dinner – tough and chewy; the weekly hot bath at the public baths; dinner for nine pence at the Civic Restaurant; standing with others in a shivering cluster at the entrance of Belsize Park Underground in London for the blast of hot air that came every two minutes as a train travelled by, in the cold long winter, gasless and lightless, of '46/'47, singing and making friends. The posters said *'It's Warmer Underground'.*

It's easy to say in retrospect, I know, but I think we were happier than today's children. At least I never heard anyone say 'I'm bored'. The word didn't exist – nor did the concept. We were just happy to be alive, and if sweets were rationed – that went on until 1953 - each one tasted the better for it.

So thank you and congratulations, all at Newcastle U3A. The book is important and the tale needs to be told: it can take some courage to give voice to the past, I know - and you have done it so vividly, and so movingly.

The snoring of a thousand men

Betty Dawson

In June 1940 I was a nine-year-old girl living in Matlock, Derbyshire. To the rear of my home was an army Drill Hall, a new building built on top of a mount with a large field in front of it. In the centre of the field was a large oval concrete road. We children would often sit on the wall and watch while some poor soldier with a full pack was marched around this road by way of a very loud sergeant major shouting out orders from the mount. Our parents told us the soldier had obviously done something wrong.

On this day in June 1940, things changed. Suddenly lots of large lorries came and deposited very dirty, tired soldiers in the field. This went on till the night and the field turned from green to khaki. There were so many soldiers. All had a kit-bag and an oblong sort of mackintosh-cum-groundsheet to lie on. The concrete road was constantly full of medical lorries and food lorries

the road was full of medical lorries

feeding the men. The medics were going round treating those with wounds and taking away those that needed better attention. The people from the houses were anxious to give them tea etc, but often the soldiers refused, as they were so well looked after by the mobile lorries. All they wanted to do was chat and sleep. Then the rain came down. The soldiers just wrapped themselves in their oblong macs and settled in for the night on the grass; they were just so glad to be safe after retreating from Dunkirk.

The children were all sent to bed, but we were woken up after a short while by a terrible noise. We thought the Germans had come, and wouldn't settle again till our father took us outside the back door to actually hear the thousands of soldiers snoring..

The next day my father had got the fire going so that my mother could have hot water (he left for work very early). Then came a knock at the door, and a very polite soldier asked if he could have a bath. He was quickly followed by two more men. When my mother said there was only enough water for one bath, the men said they would take it in turn before the water went cold. My mother was horrified but agreed. The soldiers spied my mother's copper that she used to boil our sheets in on wash day. So they filled that up and lit the fire under it. By this time more soldiers were waiting outside as word got round. After three or four soldiers had been washed, my mother insisted on cleaning the bath and refilling it with clean water. This went on all through the day. As one soldier bathed another was shaving in the kitchen. Altogether my mother reckoned about forty soldiers had used her bath that day. In the night the rattling of soldiers snoring started again. Next day bathing was again the order of the day, but not so many soldiers came, as the lorries arrived to move some on to better accommodation. They also brought others to sleep on the damp grass. It seemed to take days before the field turned green again.

Thinking back on those few days, I realised the meaning of War.

Later that year my father, who was an excellent mechanic but couldn't enlist because he had an ulcerated leg, was moved north to Shirley in Warwickshire. By day he worked as a mechanic, by night as a fireman. During this time our house was bombed twice. My parents lived for months with fibreboard for windows and candles for light at night. When raids were on they slept in the pantry under the stairs. My brother and I were evacuated to my grandmother's farm in Naseby, Northamptonshire, but I hated it and kept running away. So when the

a huge amount of bones belonging to horses and men

bombs abated a bit, my father brought me home. I can remember sitting on my dad's shoulder watching the German bombers go over, and being picked up by the ATC balloons' searchlights in a field behind our house. Then they tried to shoot them down. I don't remember being scared: I had such faith in my dad to look after me.

The night Coventry got bombed and flattened, everything changed. My dad insisted that I moved back to Naseby and stayed there until it was safe. He had got hold of enough petrol to take me there on the back of his motorbike. As we drove we passed the outskirts of Coventry. We could see a great fireball, as the Germans had used hundreds of incendiary bombs and the whole city was on fire. Then I was frightened! Also the grass verge between the two carriageways of the road was filled with armoured vehicles. My dad said they were there for when we invaded France.

When we eventually got to my gran's quiet village, Naseby, there was great excitement. One of the planes returning from Coventry had dropped its left-over bombs in fields just outside the village. It had blown a huge crater, which showed a huge amount of bones belonging to horses and men. It was then that the villagers wondered if their memorial stone to the Civil War battle was in the right place. But that is another story.

VJ Day (and what to do with a surplus bomber)

Peter Jones

I was taking School Certificate exams in 1945 so that, although VE Day provided a wonderful evening of celebration in May, we couldn't afford to have our noses far from the grindstone for long. By the end of July exams were finished and holidays had started. In early August I went with many of my friends to a school organised farming camp, 'doing our bit' to help with food production. We were encamped in a field near Market Drayton in Shropshire, almost twenty miles from our homes in The Potteries.

On 15th August we heard on the radio that Japan had surrendered, the war was completely over and VJ Day had been declared a public holiday. We were then told that we must report to our employing farmer – as I recall we were notionally paid one shilling per day, which went to the school for our food. My friend Duncan and I dutifully reported and were told: 'you must stook that field of wet barley' – a truly wretched task. Obediently we started work, and pressed on until the Land Girl came over and told us to go home and enjoy yourselves: 'I'll tell the miserable old b***** that I told you to go'. We knew that this (gorgeous) girl could twist the miserable farmer and his two miserable sons and the miserable farm-hand around her little finger, so we immediately went back to camp where we discovered that almost all our colleagues had already gone home to celebrate.

We rode our bikes like the wind along the almost empty roads, through Newcastle under Lyme to our homes in the village of Chell (the mythical Countess of Chell appears in Arnold Bennett's novels). I collected my girl friend (later my wife) and a group of friends and, as it was a beautiful sunny day, we decided to go to watch a charity cricket match (George Duckworth's XI vs Charlie Hallow's XI – some of you may remember these stalwarts of pre-war cricket) at Knypersley, about three miles away. Our convoy of bicycles soon arrived at the lovely (it still is) cricket ground. To the south is a copse of tall trees.

We established ourselves on a grassy bank beside the pavilion, lay in the sun, watched the cricket and gossiped; it was a tranquil, very English scene. Suddenly there was the roar of engines and, barely clearing the roofs of the houses to the north, a giant four-engined USAAF Liberator bomber appeared. As it dipped into the bowl of the cricket ground the players fled. The plane climbed rapidly over the trees and vanished towards the south-east. We thought that peace had returned but, a few minutes later, the plane appeared again, even lower. The players flung themselves flat on the ground in terror as the plane swooped over them. But this time as the pilot tried to pull away he couldn't climb rapidly enough. Half the tail was torn away by the trees. Smoke poured from one of the starboard engines as the wounded Liberator limped away towards the moorlands. Of course, we jumped on our bikes and rode away towards the moors to find out the fate of plane and crew. The aircraft lay on its belly in a field near Brown Edge. The two pilots and their companions (two very glamorous USAAF female officers) were unharmed and laughing and joking with the police as they awaited transportation. I realised a few weeks later why they were unconcerned at wrecking such an expensive aircraft when we went by a huge US air base in Cheshire. The war was over; bombers were no longer needed and hundreds of planes were parked on the fields waiting to be broken up and taken to the scrap yards.

A US Liberator bomber above the clouds

Many years later I heard another side of VJ Day. After my wife retired as a teacher at the Fleming Memorial Hospital she volunteered to teach English at Methodist International House in Brunswick Church. This organisation recognises that the wives especially of overseas students, doctors and company executives can be socially and linguistically isolated and provides a meeting place and a cultural and language-learning environment. My wife became friendly with a Japanese lady of similar age who told her that she had grown up in a town near the southern tip of the main island. In 1945 her father told her that he was sure the Americans would soon invade Japan and, when that occurred, he would have to kill her to avoid her falling into their hands. Early in August a rumour spread rapidly that the invasion had started but it soon became clear that it was not true; what had happened was the dropping of the atomic bombs. As she told my wife, 'I expected to die but I lived because thousands of people in Hiroshima and Nagasaki died'.

her father told her he would have to kill her

A troopship to South Africa

Aileen Smith

My mother and I left Newcastle by train for Glasgow in May 1940. We stayed in a hostel a couple of nights then boarded a ship. I can't in all honesty call it a liner, because she had been sunk in the first World War and raised again (or so we were told). Her name was ss Gloucester Castle. On leaving Glasgow we assembled with a convoy ready to set out for Cape Town. The ship had a lot of troops along with RAF families aboard, also some six nuns. It wasn't long before we couldn't keep up with the convoy, so we were left to fend for ourselves. [1]

We had a cabin which we shared with a very nice Mrs Fox, who came from Birmingham. I was on the top, Mum on the bottom and Mrs Fox on the other side. Many of the cabins had been knocked into bigger areas and many families shared them. Being classed as a troopship, the space was

ss Gloucester Castle

very limited. The first class lounge was for ladies and children during the day and we were allowed on deck for walks and games. The wives organised bingo and bridge, singing entertainment and various activities. Children were taken in hand by the nuns, and I remember Sister Mary Francis teaching us girls (about a dozen of us) to tapdance, chanting 'scuffle, step, stamp, spring' over and over again. They also taught us lessons each morning. The news was broadcast throughout the ship every morning at 5am and evening at 6pm. The day's speed and journey was announced and we had a big map, made by the nuns, and recorded our progress daily.

One night we heard that we would be arriving at Cantilena sometime the next day, but we anchored in the roads and weren't allowed ashore, as some epidemic was raging on the island. We stayed a few days taking water and supplies aboard and set off again, following the coast until we reached Assertion Isle, where two of the nuns left us.

---

[1] *Editor's note: Tragically the ss Gloucester Castle was sunk off the south west coast of Africa two years later, on the 15th July 1942, with a loss of 93 passengers and crew.*

The weather was getting so hot that the troops started to sleep on deck and we used their hammock room as a dining room. We weren't allowed on deck after 9pm. One day early in the morning we sighted a raft. Men were waving to us. As the time went on, rumours flew through the ship: it was a raft on which the men were alive – or they were dead - all sorts of wild explanations. As the day went on and we got nearer to the raft, it turned out to be a dead whale, belly up

a dead whale belly up

and stinking. When we crossed the Equator all the crew dressed up as pirates. There was a big blow-up pool used for us children, but that day at noon the ship's officers and army officers were all tipped in. We had a party that night, singing on the deck.

After some weeks we had news over the ship's telegraph that we didn't have enough coal to get to Cape Town and were going to put in at Walvis Bay (South West Africa, now Namibia). We made the coast and anchored in a quiet bay, then were towed into the dockside. We were allowed ashore the next day. Walvis Bay was exactly like an old town in the cowboy films, with a sandy road straight down the middle of the town and duckboard pavements on both sides. The next day a few of the mums and kids went on a train ride along the coast to another town called Swaquamund. The train followed the coast, and on the straight stretch the driver came down the carriages (rather like a tram) and took our fares. Along the coast-line we saw flocks of pink flamingos wading in the shallows, pink because the sea was rich in little shrimps. When we arrived at the end of the line, we had iced lemonade and water-melons, then returned to the dock and once more set sail for Cape Town

As we docked at Cape Town after our voyage of three months and two days, every one was looking for their husbands. The troops were disembarked first, and we were taken to a hotel. It was very old-fashioned, all leather and lights. As the only train up country didn't leave until Tuesday we had from Friday to explore Cape Town. On Sunday we went up Table Mountain, climbing up General Smuts Sunday Walk. As this was a bit too much for us, on Monday Mum and I went up by cable car. On the top you could see for miles, but then the 'tablecloth' came down and we had to leave.

We had a cable from Dad saying he would meet us in Gwelo on Friday night. Mum learnt later that Dad thought we were with a convoy that had left two weeks after us but had suffered heavy losses on its way. He had only been told we were safe and in Capetown too late make any arrangements to meet

Dad thought our convoy had suffered losses

us. The train made the trip twice a week, Tuesday up and Friday down. This time we had a couchette to ourselves. Meals were served in the dining car and the steward brought our beds made up every night. On leaving the Cape we went through the Garden of Eden, a vast stretch of plateau covered with flowers of every colour and sorts. Then later at night we went though the Kalahari Desert. This was horrible with dust everywhere, choking heat and very unpleasant. Often we stopped at a station (a signpost) with milk churns and natives selling goods and fruit. Many a time the train just stopped in the middle of nowhere. We arrived at our first town of any size, Durban, where the train split in two, one half going on to Lourenco Marques and the other up to Southern Rhodesia (now Zimbabwe) via Whitehall and Bulawayo, and then on to Gwelo (our stop). After that it continued to the capital, Salisbury. The train took three days to get to Bulawayo then another night to Gwelo, our destination at last. Dad was on the platform waiting for us.

We lived in an old bank building at first then moved out to Guinea Fowl Married Quarters beside the RAF camp where my dad was stationed. The camp trained young pilots to fly using Tiger Moths. When we first moved in, there was nothing much to entertain the families, but soon a tennis court and small clubhouse were built on site. We went to school in Gwelo travelling by bus (made out of a lorry) every day, eleven miles in and eleven miles out. School started at 8 and finished at 12.30. We spent most afternoons at the camp swimming pool. One of our best entertainments was the bioscope. Part of a hanger was partitioned off and benches were put at the back for ordinary ranks, chairs next for corporals and sergeants, with basket seats in the front for officers. We kids used the side and pinched the officers' seats. We also took pillows and blankets with us, as the hanger was so cold. Films were shown on Tuesday, Thursday and Saturday nights. In the interval the cookhouse provided ice cream at a tickey a tub (3d, about 1p). The films did the rounds of the three camps, Thornhill, Hodnet and Guinea Fowl, so often we got the same film a few weeks later. We went on leave to the Victoria Falls, another time to the Birchnough Bridge, which is a copy of the Tyne Bridge, and also went to the Zimbabwe ruins. We had a short holiday in Bulawayo and the Motopus Hills, and another in Salisbury.

At Christmas all the huts and messes would put up decorations, with the prize of a barrel of beer for the best. They used blankets and palm-leaves, upturned beds and anything else, but always with a bar. The judging was done after church parade on Christmas morning, and by the end of the day no-one was sober. The camp always put on a Christmas party for us kids. I remember the magician asking my Dad for his watch, wrapping it up and hammering it with a hammer and then running off. Dad did get his watch back later when it was found in a jelly.

Shared beds and shared schools

Dorothy M Jawthrop

I was eight years old when war was declared on that never-to-be-forgotten Sunday in September. I was out in the lane with my skipping rope when that very first wail of the siren was heard over the town and I can remember a panicky feeling in my tummy as I rushed inside, and straight up the stairs to bring down all my family's gas masks. I was so sure that the German aeroplanes would be over us any minute and that the bombing and gassing would start immediately. My mum, dad and older brother were sitting around the wireless with very serious faces but they did manage a smile when they saw me standing there telling them to put on their gas masks. Fortunately they were never needed.

Digging a hole in the back garden for an Anderson shelter: Sylvia, age 9, with a man-sized spade and boyfriend

We were lucky to live in Hexham which was considered to be a safe place, but the preparations for war were much the same as anywhere else. Those flat-roofed, red brick air-raid shelters had been built at the end of the school yards, and some people had dug deep down in their gardens to make their own Anderson Shelters, covering them with curved corrugated roofs, and topping them with sand bags or sods of grass. We didn't have one, but we were prepared to go under the stairs if it should become necessary. It never did.

We were all encouraged to 'Dig for Victory' so lots of flower beds became vegetable patches. The gardeners were mostly women, as the men had gone off to fight in the war. In the autumn, we were asked to go out and pick rose hips. They were taken to schools and other centres where they were weighed and we were paid for each pound collected. They were rich in vitamin C and were made into juice for babies and young children as there were no imports of fruit such as oranges.

Soon the evacuees came to Hexham. Lots of frightened, bewildered children from Newcastle were herded into church halls where the worthy ladies of the WVS tried their best to find them suitable homes.

frightened, bewildered children

It must have been a heart-rending task. Very few of them settled into their strange new homes and a life in the country and most of them had returned home before the bombing really started. My grandma had a brother and sister from Byker. They were just a little younger than me, but we really couldn't understand each other; it was hopeless! They didn't like our food and they screamed when they were put in the bath. It was not a happy situation. Everything was just too different for them, so they preferred to risk the bombs back in their own homes.

One day when I came home from school my mum said two ladies had called to have a look around our house and had decided that we had room for an evacuee. She came with others from Tynemouth High School and to me she was a big girl. She was fourteen and I was only nine. I thought Nancy was wonderful. She had lovely strong blondish hair, the sort that never went flat in the damp like mine, which was brown and fine. We shared a three-quarter sized bed and every night I used to lie and watch her, fascinated, as she very deftly twisted her hair into those little pin curls before we settled for sleep. My mum, years afterwards, used to wonder what had possessed her to put the two of us in the small single bedroom while my brother, Jack (eight years my senior), had quite a large double room all to himself. We came to the conclusion that it was most likely because he would soon have to go off to the war and so she wanted to spoil him while she could. Jack and Nancy were just at the age of having enormous appetites and my poor mum had no easy task in making the meagre rations spin out. They would have eaten everyone's butter ration for the week in one go, given half a chance, so she gave them each a dish with their 2oz portion which they marked out into seven days – they had great games watching whose would last the longest.

Tynemouth High School and Hexham Grammar School shared the school day, the locals going in the mornings while the Tynemouth pupils went in the afternoons. The next week everything was reversed. The system seemed to work very well and when eventually the Tynemouth school returned home some evacuees, whose parents had come to stay in Hexham for the duration of the war, continued on at Hexham School and many long lasting friendships were made. In fact I am still regularly in touch with a friend in Cullercoats.

The day came when my brother went off into the navy. He had always wanted to go to sea so, to make sure, he volunteered at the age of seventeen. My parents were very upset but all the sons, brothers and some dads had to go. Families were torn apart, some for ever. We were lucky. Jack

icy convoys to Russia

came through unscathed although he had some hairy moments on the convoys to Russia, particularly in the long winters when the weather conditions were indescribable. He told us tales of the huge waves lashing over the decks and immediately turning to ice. I remember we used to knit sea-boot stockings in oiled wool for him, but oh what a sticky mess the wool made of your hands! Nevertheless I think they were appreciated. Years later a strange coincidence took place. I was entertaining a few friends one Christmas and I introduced Jack to our village doctor. They got talking about their time in the Royal Navy and realised they had both been on the Russian convoys at roughly the same time. The doctor asked Jack which destroyer he was on and when Jack said 'HMS Middleton' he gasped and said 'I can't believe it! The men on that ship picked me up after our destroyer was torpedoed.'

My brother also spent time with the North Atlantic convoys. The merchant ships bringing essential goods from America needed protection from the German U-boats, battle ships and constant air attacks. They were very dangerous waters. Whilst in New York he was befriended by an American who entertained him in great style and started sending food parcels to us in England. Looking back it is quite amazing that we did actually receive them. Opening them up was magic. I also remember Jack's trips home on leave and that wonderful kitbag. Amongst his clothes and personal belongings there were small presents from strange lands. It was out of that kitbag that I received my very first pair of nylon stockings – all the way from New York.

I suppose Jack was quite lucky as he also spent time in South Africa while his ship was being re-fitted in Capetown. Once again he met someone who was so very kind and with whom he still keeps in touch. However, these were just a few lighter incidents in what was a terrible war. He was there at the D-day landings but never spoke much about it.

There were lots of soldiers billeted in and around Hexham and I can remember the minister of our church asking from the pulpit if any of the ladies would be willing to give baths to one or two each week. There was a great response and lists were made and we were to have two soldiers every Friday night. How I looked forward to these bath nights. We had a fire-back boiler and I can remember the hot water rumbling up through the pipes to the bathroom. How hot we were in the summer, but it was lovely in the winter and the soldiers really

soldiers brought the wider world into our lives

enjoyed sitting round the fire eating sandwiches and home-made cake and enjoying a few home comforts. They brought a bit of the wider world into our lives and we all enjoyed the sharing experience.

We felt reasonably safe living in Hexham, but we could see the searchlights sweeping across the sky, hear the thump of the bombs as they fell on Newcastle and see the orange glow in the sky from the fires. One night we did have a scary moment. The German planes used to fly over us on their way to bomb Glasgow and this particular night we heard the drone of their engines as they returned. Then, horror of horrors, the whole street was alight. They had dropped a flare. My mum and I were alone at the time and we clung together as we watched and waited. We didn't have long to wait. Soon we heard the drone of a lone plane coming nearer and nearer and we were certain that it was going to drop its last remaining bombs on us. I can still feel the fear now. We seemed paralysed. We should have gone under our stairs, but we just stood there and waited. Then the plane changed direction and we saw the stick of bombs fall over the countryside up the North Tyne Valley. Great was our relief. We heard later that the bombs had fallen in some fields near the village of Wall without causing any damage.

During the early part of the war, long wooden huts (Nissen huts) sprang up. There were some on Tyne Green, used for a short time to house Italian prisoners of war. Some were erected in the countryside out of the town and were used as a holiday camp for children from the bombed areas of Tyneside, but the biggest of all became the Hexham Emergency Hospital. Wounded soldiers, sailors and airmen were treated here, and it soon became a familiar sight to see local volunteers pushing wheel-chairs and beds about the town and through the park in order to help the recovery of the wounded men. We were all asked to knit small squares which were stitched together to make blankets for the hospital and any surplus was sent to similar hospitals in other parts of the country.

German prisoners-of-war.....

There was a camp in the grounds of Featherstone Castle, just outside Haltwhistle. Again, Nissen huts were erected and became the home for German prisoners of war. We weren't very aware of this camp until the war in Europe was over when the prisoners were given a little freedom. They began to be seen working on farms, in nursery gardens and in allotments (under guard of course). During their incarceration they had formed concert parties and choirs and now they were taken, under supervision, to the surrounding towns and villages to entertain the local people. A friend of mine remembers a wonderful concert given in Hexham Abbey by their choir.

.....in the church choir

Our Methodist church at that time had a very good choir but, like all choirs, was short of men, so the Germans were given permission to join us and swell the depleted ranks of the tenors and basses. Their leader was a brilliant organist and it was a treat to hear him fill the church with music. I remember once they took the whole service. It was quite a difficult situation as many people in the town had lost husbands and sons and here was the enemy mixing a little within the community. Fortunately, to my knowledge, there was no trouble and some friendships were made which have lasted for a lifetime. They had been very well treated as prisoners and were probably very pleased to give something back to the British people who had treated them so well. Quite a few were not too happy about returning home.

May 8th 1945 was the day on which the war in Europe came to an end, and later that summer we had our first holiday for five years. We went to Tynemouth for a week but, oh dear, it all looked so desolate. The coils of barbed wire were still on the beaches. Lots of buildings were partly destroyed; some were reduced to just heaps of rubble while some had no roofs at all. I remember that one house on the front in Whitley Bay had had its front wall blown away; yet hanging from the ceiling was an electric light apparently still intact. One of the saddest sights of all, though, was to see the wrecks of ships both in the mouth of the river and in the sea. I think we counted about fifteen. It is hard to believe, when looking out over the mouth of the Tyne today, that it was once such a scene of devastation. How wonderful it is to live where there is peace in the world.

The war years had all been a huge sacrifice for so many, and we must never allow ourselves to forget that time as we enjoy the wonderful freedom that we have today.

Bombers over the Thames

David Woodroff

For almost all of the duration of World War Two, I was growing up in Kingston upon Thames. During the first phase of what people called 'the phoney war' from September 1939 to May 1940, little disturbed the peaceful way of life we were used to. In the riverside town, our first experience was watching the armada of small boats going down river heading for the beaches of Dunkirk to take part in the rescue of what remained of the British Expeditionary Force. On their return, those boats discharged their cargo of weary and grimy soldiers into makeshift camps and their arrival

Hurricane Fighter

caught the attention of the local population who wondered what was to follow. We did not have long to wait before the aerial battle for Britain began. That summer of 1940 became the background for the sight and sounds of German bombers being pursued by British fighter aircraft in their defence of the targets around London. As a lad I have a vivid memory of standing on top of an air raid shelter in the school playground watching a low flying German Heinkel being chased by three Hurricane fighters. The German rear gunner shot down the first of the fighters and also the second one who pressed home his attack. Bravely, the third Hurricane followed on and the bomber was brought down in the park and I heard its bomb load explode. The whole engagement lasted no more than 30 seconds from first sighting until the final explosion.

A few months later I had another experience along with several school friends on our way home on our bikes. The afternoon was foggy and suddenly a bomber broke through the mist just behind us. It was so low that we could see the face of a crew member as the bomber passed over us and the rear gunner sprayed a short burst of machine gun fire across the road ahead of us. We all fell off our bikes with the surprise but nobody was hurt and the bomber vanished back into the mist. It was widely held that German air crews used the River Thames as a navigational aid to reach their London targets. My school lay between the river and the Hawker Aircraft Factory where Hurricane fighters were built. This lone bomber may well have thought we were a group of workers from that factory. Anyway, we all got safely away.

Thirteen schools

June Brown

I was ten years old when war was declared against Germany. I remember going out into the yard of our house in West Hartlepool to listen to the first practice of an air raid warning, so we could recognise it, I suppose.

I also remember coming home from school with a list of items I had to take so that I could be evacuated and was most upset when my Dad said I couldn't go. This was the start of what was called the 'phoney war', because children were being evacuated into the country, away from towns and cities where air raids were expected, and being put into houses with total strangers. At the beginning of the war everyone thought Germany would start dropping bombs on British cities, but in fact this happened much later.

It also meant that schools were closed part of the time. I distinctly remember going to the house of one of our teachers for a lesson. I can still see her, Miss Anderson, with very white hair, offering us sweets or cakes from a tiered cake stand, and we thought it was great. We were all due to take our 11+ exams and this was one way of keeping up with our lessons. I never did sit that exam, which meant I couldn't go to a grammar school because Dad had moved down to Cornwall and we packed up our furniture and returned to Wallsend waiting to join him. However, before any move was made to go south Dad said we were staying put because a German submarine

A German submarine had been washed up

had been washed up in Falmouth and he decided it was probably more dangerous down south than it was in the north.

It was whilst living in Wallsend that we really did have air raids. I was taken outside one night to see a German plane caught in the glare of searchlights, with the sound of the big guns which finally brought it down. When the air raid siren went we had to put on our siren suits (a long-legged, one-piece outfit with a long zip like a baby-grow - even Winston Churchill wore one). As we lived in a terraced house we had to go along several streets to the nearest public air-raid shelter. This was underground, very dark and cold, with long benches along each side. Again, we only reappeared when the 'all-clear' went, and we used to hope this didn't happen before midnight, because we wouldn't have to go to school the next day. Alternative Anderson air-raid shelters were available if you had a garden but these were very wet and damp.

Shortly after that we moved to Manchester and it was here that we suffered the worst air raids. We lived near the docks where Dad worked and we were sharing a house with another family from Wallsend. This house was huge, with attics and cellars and we lived on the top floor. The house was furnished with beautiful antique furniture and very thick carpets. I remember the fun we had with a big roll-top desk with lots of little drawers and cubby-holes. There was a winding fire escape on our floor which had a huge cherry tree alongside it. Needless to say, the cherries didn't last long.

When an air raid started we had to go down several flights of stairs with lots of glass windows. The air raids were happening every night, so Dad and his mate brought several long

the raids were getting worse and we never seemed to sleep through them

pit props and fixed them into the middle of the cellar ceiling to help support the roof. All the beds were taken down into the biggest room and we slept there every night. The raids were getting worse and we never seemed to sleep through them. I could always recognise the sound of German planes – they had a particular drone - and it always woke me up. We could hear bombs dropping near us and Dad made us go into the middle of the room under the supported ceiling, with blankets wrapped round us, until the raid was over.   That really was very frightening. We eventually returned to Wallsend, so once again I had another change of schooling. I once worked out that I made 13 changes of school before I started work at 16.

I remember how, when we lived on a farm at Gilsland, miles out into the country in Cumberland, a German plane came over and dropped a bomb on the moors - apparently because a farmer had been using a lantern outside. It was a very desolate area and had never had an air raid before, but I can still see my Dad looking out of the window that night because we had both recognised the sound of a German plane and then we heard the thump as the bomb was dropped. It was the talk of the village as it was their first experience of bombing.

In Gilsland we were living in a small cottage with no electricity or gas, lighting was by paraffin lamps and cooking was by means of open fire and oven. It was very primitive and we had no toilet inside - this was outside - and no, you couldn't flush it away. We had to dig a hole in the garden and empty it regularly - no wonder the vegetables grew so well.   The allowance of 12oz sweets, though, was very hard on children. Can you imagine them liking this – about one Mars bar per week? I can remember getting a shoe box full of chocs and sweets which Dad had sent. At this time he was working in Southampton and he had made friends with a man who had a sweet shop – trust Dad! He had a very sweet tooth (he even used to pinch our ration) so he made up for this with boxes of sweets.

Dad used to get a train each weekend from Newcastle to Low Row and then walk another two miles to our cottage at the Banks. He always brought a big empty suitcase with him and we would fill it up with eggs and rabbit skins (to make gloves and mitts) and, of course, the odd rabbit he'd caught himself. I sometimes went with him to the station when he was returning using my bike as a carrier.

Bikes in fact were our only means of transport. There were no buses and I cycled every day to school at Brampton, about four miles away. The Banks was very aptly named - a few pedals and I was off down a big hill to Lanercost and then a long climb to Brampton. If we wanted to go to the pictures in Brampton it was bikes out again and I would do the same on a Sunday to get Dad's newspapers - surely a labour of love.

I can remember sweet rationing ending in 1953. I was working in an office in Northumberland Street and I was given a shopping order from the rest of the staff to buy sweets from Maynard's. I believe that the shop ran out of stock in a few hours. When I am shopping now and see the overflowing trolleys I wonder how we'd manage if food were ever to be scarce again.

A bomb in our garden

Marguerite Rook

I was born in Maryport, on the West Cumberland coast in 1928 and was 11 when the war broke out. I can remember that, after Baptist Church Sunday School, I had gone to a lady's house to pick up some cigarette cards which we were collecting. She had the radio on and the news came on to announce that we were at war with Germany.

But nothing happened to begin with. It wasn't until 22 July 1940 that the reality of war touched us. I remember the day well as it was my mother's birthday. A stray bomber came over (there was no warning) and dropped a bomb in our garden. There was a huge crater and glass from the windows all over the floor, but I was more concerned about our cats, Joseph and Topsy. Although she was very old Topsy was okay, but sadly Joseph had been killed. As the gas was off we couldn't make a cup of tea and had to go to the Freemasons' Hall, where they were dispensing cups of tea to those families affected by the bomb blast. Mum was crying, which was the first time I'd seen that, so it made quite an impression on me.

That night there were 12 people killed in a town of 12,000 inhabitants. Every death is tragic, but one case was particularly sad. A young teacher had brought a group of evacuees to Maryport from South Shields. Liking the area and believing it would be safer than South Shields, she had gone back to collect her mother. Both of them were killed that night. Another poignant occasion was when I saw an Austrian family, who had fled to Maryport to find safety, walking up the street with their few belongings as their home had been bombed.

Although Maryport wasn't a prime target for the German bombers, it was on the flight path to Glasgow and the planes would often loose their load on Maryport rather than return to Germany with bombs still on board. We used to go under the table during air raids. Mines were dropped on Silloth and incendiaries on Broughton Moor, both nearby. We got to know the sound of the planes' engines.

praying for the school to be bombed

I felt a bit guilty when our school was bombed as I'd been praying for Hitler to bomb the school so we wouldn't have to go to lessons. I was foiled as this didn't mean that school was cancelled: instead we shared the National Anglican School buildings, taking it in turns to go to school in the morning or afternoon.

Later I progressed to a mixed grammar school in Cockermouth, although most of the male teachers were in the Forces. I had to go to school on the bus. This used to pass a truck taking the prisoners of war to work from their camp and we always used to wave to them. The Italian prisoners always waved back, but the Germans never did. At school we used to have air raid drills to see how fast we could get to the trenches in the playing fields. This was always a welcome break as it got us out of lessons.

was he the German pilot ?

Occasionally we used to cycle the eight miles to school and one day my friend Betty and I were cycling back home when an airman caught up with us. His uniform looked slightly different and when I queried this with him he said it was the Czech airforce. I said that there were a lot of Czechs in Maryport and he asked to be shown where one lived. Betty had got a bit scared and cycled on ahead of us. As we approached Maryport we came across a crowd of people looking at a German aircraft which had crashed. The airman seemed to be getting agitated and I pointed him in the direction of the first Czech house. I have since wondered if he had actually been the pilot of the German plane who had parachuted out before his plane crashed.

Clothes were rationed, which is hard when you're growing up in your teens. However we developed our own fashion trends. We were all issued with gas masks which we had to take to school, so there was a fashion for gas mask holders. Initially I had a cube box, then a handbag shape with a purse on the side and then a shoulder bag with purse. We also had to have ID discs and another fashion trend was for a bracelet or necklace with your ID disc. My family had American relatives and they used to send us parcels which contained Tangy lipstick and hairclips which were joyously received. Also my bother, Don, who was in the Fleet Air Arm, had to go to America for training and when he came back he brought with him nylons and other gifts much to our delight.

Life seemed to go on even during the war – it wasn't all doom. There were always plenty of dances, parties and musical events. We used to have

rexine box and gas mask

'Save Britain' concerts

'Save Britain' concerts in Maryport and it was at one of these recitals that my aunt introduced me to Kathleen Ferrier, the greatest lyric contralto that England has produced. Later I used to sing at these concerts too.

Sadly we were always hearing about people getting telegrams telling them a loved one had died, or was missing. One of these was my cousin Billy, who was killed in Italy at Mount Casino not long after his wedding, at which I had sung. Unfortunately war doesn't always bring out the best in people and some people didn't treat those in protected occupations very well. There were also rumours in the town that the Italians running the ice cream parlour were sending money back to Italy to support Mussolini, which resulted in some people throwing stones at the shop window.

Food was another commodity that was rationed, but we had a well balanced diet and there was sufficient to eat. Butter and meat were rationed but as my family liked offal we could always get an ox tail, cow heel and tripe, which weren't rationed. (I couldn't eat meat until I was about 15 when I started school meals). Living by the sea my father used to go fishing to augment our diet. At school we used to get a third of a pint of milk for which we had to pay 2½d (about 0.5p), although those who couldn't afford it got ½ pint milk free with digestive biscuits. For Christmas we would get a capon from the farm (we would have to pluck it before we could cook it) and one year we celebrated the New Year with kippers.

Even during the war I found it hard to reconcile the fact that both sides were praying to the same God for victory, disregarding Jesus' commandment to 'love thine enemy'. At the end of the day families from both sides lost loved ones and many innocent people were killed.

Evacuees came and went

Alec Bamford

In September 1939, we had a second-hand Pye wireless, but it was away to be repaired. In order to keep my father informed, since it was sunny and warm my mother sat knitting by our gate, under a rambling cream rose to listen to the news coming through the open door and window from a couple who were both quite deaf.

As the days went by we were issued with gas masks, then many of the village turned out to see the arrival of a coach-load or two of children. There were enough for the school to need an extra teacher for the Infants, a Mrs Brown who came with the evacuees. The Headmaster was in charge of 'Dad's Army'. Some evacuees went back quite quickly: of those who remained, a few stayed after the end of the war and made their home in our village.

When the sweets came in, we rushed to one of our shops before our favourites sold out. Perhaps it was once a month that there was a stream of people going to Mrs Reynolds' (clean) outhouse; she was in her WVS uniform distributing meat or pork pies.

Do you remember cod liver oil? I had no trouble downing a spoon of that, but I thought cod liver oil and malt had a vile taste.

A friend of my mother ate all the cheese allowance at one sitting – perhaps her husband had most of the meat.

Only once did we have anything to do with bombs; we went up the hill about a quarter of a mile and examined the craters – 15 of them in a line, one in each field and missing the road. As far as I know this was the one and only time there was an attempt to bomb the steelworks in the nearby town.

I have a memory of seeing double-decker buses towing what looked like a brazier on wheels to provide coal gas for the engine; this brazier was only tried out on a few routes. Recently I heard of someone whose family car had a large bag of gas on the roof in order to save petrol.

The lovely mellow stone houses in parts of Northamptonshire are built from local ironstone, but it is a poor quality source of iron. With imports much reduced, many quarries were opened around where I lived. The stone was crushed, piled in heaps over a fire, and steamed and smoked away until it was a dark red-brown and ready for use in furnaces. Three towns locally had blast furnaces, and some of the ore was taken by train to Middlesborough. There was also the day when men came to cut down the chapel railings and take them away for recycling.

Realising the meaning of war

Joan Barker

The day war broke out I was just two months short of my sixth birthday. We spent that day having lunch and tea with friends of my parents who lived in a railway carriage. I think our church choir and theirs were joining forces for their choir festival. The novelty of people living in a railway carriage took my attention far more than the news that had come over the wireless at 11 o'clock that morning.

It wasn't long before my father was away, and I realised that life was changing. I just seemed to accept everything that was happening. I wasn't afraid. I just did as I was told. I lived with Mother at home on the outskirts of Nottingham for some time, but we couldn't use the shelter that Dad had made for us in the garden, as it was too damp. We didn't have much of a problem apart from the noise of Big Beth, the large gun which was stationed not far from us. We had a lot of shrapnel shaking the guttering, and for most of the war that was all that worried us when we were at home.

the noise of Big Beth

However we did stay quite a lot of the time with my mother's sister, and it was there that I began to understand a bit more about what war meant. Uncle was an ARP Warden, and every time there was a siren sounding he would fetch the elderly lady next door to go into the cellar with us. She would sit on the steps sobbing: 'Those boys, those

40

boys'. It wasn't long before I realised that her concern was for all those men who'd been called to fight for their country, whether they believed it was right or wrong. It made a big impression on me. I didn't have any fears till later on in the war and my understanding got a lot better. When we had the doodlebugs towards the end of the war, I was the first one to get to the head of the cellar steps. I'd never bothered before.

We had very strict rules at school: how you behaved when the sirens sounded; the crocodiles in which you walked properly to the shelters; our own spots in the shelter; always travelling to and from school in threes.

school rules in threes

I think it must have been in the summer in Nottingham towards the end of the war when I was the last one of the three to be picked up for school from my house. The siren sounded as my two friends arrived at the door. We dived under the table in the living-room as we'd been told to do at school, to get under a bed or table if we couldn't get to the shelter. We called for my mother to come with us. However we looked up out of the window and saw a plane being shot down by Big Beth.

We were very quiet on our way to school. I think it was dawning on us just what war meant.

On VE Day in 1945 I was amazed that Mother was so happy to take me that evening and walk to the city centre where everybody was celebrating. We could have lights on; we could have bells ringing; we could make as much noise as we liked. That was absolutely wonderful.

That was the end of the war. We were fortunate. Nottingham did have some direct hits, but nothing as much as other people suffered. We were grateful for that. It left an impression that is still with me now.

Two waves of evacuation

Irene Taylor

The day before war was declared (I was 10 years old), my elementary school was evacuated to Carlisle, a place I had never heard of nor visited. The children all congregated, along with their mothers, in the school hall and as much information as was available was imparted to the anxious mothers. Each child carried a gas mask, a satchel or haversack with their clothes and a carrier bag (survival kit) with, among other things, a piece of fruit, a packet of biscuits and a bar of chocolate. I was particularly proud of my gas mask case, which had been custom made in real leather by my father and stood out among the scores of standard cardboard boxes. We walked in a crocodile accompanied by our teachers through the long streets of terraced houses to Walker station. The streets were lined with mothers and other relatives of the children; many were weeping, others cheering and waving Union Jacks. We all felt very important if a little apprehensive. Being an easily distracted child, I became separated from my group in Carlisle station and was rescued by a teacher with a group from a different school. I learnt later that my own teacher, who was responsible for the class, had been distraught and spent a sleepless night until we were reunited the next day.

I was billeted with three other girls in a boarding house run by two sisters who regarded evacuees as a source of income and showed little interest in us. As soon as we arrived, we were taken to the bathroom where we were told to get into the bath together and, not having met these girls before my modesty was greatly offended. The next morning all the adults and children gathered around the wireless and heard Mr Chamberlain solemnly announce to the nation that we were at war with Germany. Seeing the grave faces of the adults, I realised that this was very serious but did not understand the full consequences and it had little impact on me.

Mothers and children under school age were included in the second wave of evacuation and, in due course, my mother arrived with my sister aged two. Discovering my whereabouts, she decided to find a place where we could be together. She achieved this by walking the streets of a strange town with a toddler in a pushchair knocking on doors indiscriminately. Her efforts were eventually rewarded when a kind lady who lived on her own said she was going to stay with her sister for the duration of the war and that we could live in her house as long as we wished. My mother never forgot this lady's kindness and for the next three months we settled in at number 1 Fusehill Street which happened to be opposite the workhouse in a not very salubrious area. The house was one of several built in a square around a courtyard at the back with a communal tap in the middle of the yard, as there was no running water in the houses. There was gas light downstairs but not upstairs and we went to bed with a candle. We all slept in the same bedroom and my mother and I used to giggle when we undressed as the static in our under slips set off a shower of sparks in the dim light.

our slips let off sparks

Unlike children who stayed in Newcastle, we had full-time schooling but had plenty of time after school to explore our new environment. I remember the craze of the time was a round bat with a ball on a piece of elastic, the idea being to see how many times you could bounce the ball off the bat. This occupied us for many happy hours.

After a few weeks, my father came to see us bringing with him a canary in a cage. This must have been quite difficult to transport on the train and bus and I can only assume that either I had at some time carelessly expressed a wish to own a canary or that he thought the house had faulty gas appliances.

After a few months, a lot of the women (including my mother) decided to return home. This was partly because, in spite of dire predictions, all the industrial cities had not been wiped out by the Luftwaffe and partly because their men folk, who were in reserved occupations, were working very long hours and unused to looking after themselves. So when their initial fears had been allayed for the time being, they returned home to face whatever was in store together. The Anderson shelter was installed, ration books were distributed, my father joined the ARP and we raised chickens and grew vegetables to eke out the rations. I resumed my education albeit half time and, having passed the scholarship examination, gained a place at the Convent of the Sacred Heart grammar school which, of course, had been evacuated to Kendal. So off I went again to spend two (I have to say idyllic) years in the Lake District.

Farm life in the Scottish Borders

Margaret Smedley

I arrived in this world in the middle of an air raid on the nearby munitions factory at Gretna. Unfortunately the Maternity Hospital was loath to open its doors during the blackout, but did so reluctantly after learning that my parents had travelled some distance to get there.

Living on a farm meant that we did not experience the real hardships of food shortages as we were allowed to keep back a certain quantity of our produce. I do remember visiting aunts in Glasgow and taking fresh eggs, which they pounced on with glee, although it was very puzzling to me that they were going to put them into isinglass to preserve them.

eggs preserved in isinglass

An aunt and uncle lived in Clydebank with a large family. As the shipbuilding areas were bombed frequently, it was decided to evacuate the children to the countryside. Consequently our Clydebank cousins came to us and other relatives, and I think I must have been a very spoilt toddler as they were all much older. I'm sure my mother was never short of babysitters.

My eldest cousin told me a lovely story recently about this period of her life. While working in the shipyards, her father made her a little ring from scrap metal. She wore this all the time when on the farm, but one day she lost it when helping a neighbour to feed hay to his cattle. After searching carefully she left in tears but the farmer comforted her and told her to return next day when nature would have taken its course. Sure enough he presented her with the ring next day, so all was well. If only that ring could talk!

spare bedrooms requisitioned by the officers

Another event which looms large in my memory is when a company of soldiers camped out on the farm. Spare bedrooms were requisitioned by the officers and the outbuildings taken over for cooking and other tasks. This must have been quite an upheaval for my parents, as the everyday farm jobs still had to be done and their routine would be greatly upset. When they eventually left, my mother was given an old silk parachute. Guess who had the best silk petticoats during the war-years shortages!

There was a prisoner of war camp in our area and each day a lorry arrived with men from the camp to do farm work. Being small, I was not aware of their position and only knew that they liked to play with us. No doubt they were missing their own children back home. I remember a very nice German called Johann who drew fabulous pictures on our bothy walls. I was also rescued by a lorry load of Ukrainians when I fell off my bike on the way home from school.

All in all, my war memories seem very exciting, especially the sight of large tanks trundling along small country roads. When I read about the blitz and food queues, I realise how relatively well off I was living in the countryside.

Recycling is 'in the blood'

Hilary Worthy

Recycling is now official policy and 'the thing', but to those of us who grew up in wartime, it is 'in the blood'. Anyone who saves rubber bands, pieces of string and wrapping paper, or who uses for shopping lists or rough notes the back of paper which is written or printed on one side only, shows the wartime touch.

Some measures were more drastic, like the re-footing of lisle stockings from the legs of other pairs. Going to college was only achieved by letting out seams on an outgrown tweed suit, and making a housecoat from a blanket. Unravelling knotted jumpers worn at the cuffs or elbows could then provide wool to be re-knitted into smaller objects like gloves or scarves, and save precious clothing coupons. Evenings were occupied with the endless darning of school lisle stockings in the pre-nylon era.

The kitchen was another area for ingenious economy, such as using malt as a sugar substitute in cooking, and recipes without eggs or adapting them to dried egg powder. Mixing butter or margarine with milk in a hand-held churn made it go further. Cooking the overnight porridge in a home-made hay box saved fuel. Nothing was thrown away without considering if it might have an alternative use or be handed down to a smaller relation.

The joy of envelopes

Mo Morgan

I could draw in one corner all the sights of the streaks and the flashes of light that silhouetted the cranes over the fields towards the river. I could write the words for the sounds of the 'crashes and bangs' that accompanied those amazing lights, and I could make comforting patterns all round the edges to keep my paper safe. I could marvel at the little sketches my mum made of our hens and the eggs they laid for my tea and the rhyme she wrote down about my not having had an egg since Sunday, and now it was half past three; and we chuckled, singing it together from the words she had written. I

47

could draw a picture of me looking down from the top bunk in the air-raid shelter at three smiling faces looking up at me from their game of bridge and the fourth player craning her neck from the nearside of the table beneath me to say: 'Hello, did that last noisy aeroplane wake you up?'

It felt such a contented and happy time with family and neighbours all around supporting and helping each other.

No wonder I still save all my envelopes. I use them, cut into pieces, for sticking onto those foil paracetamol eights to note what time I took them; to stick on freezer packs with the date cooked and frozen; for message pads by the phones; for little missives to my mum who can't remember how to boil eggs now, or whether she should be waiting for the Day Centre bus or the carer to come to keep her company and make her meal for her.

Perhaps my favourite use is to tear the envelope diagonally across the cleanest corner just the right size to fit it over the page of the book I am reading. As well as keeping my place by moving it onto the next page as I am reading, I can keep a note of any of the characters or words to look up or vital parts of the plot or quotations that I want to remember. If there is a map to refer to at the front or a glossary at the back, then separate envelope corners mark their places. If one corner is filled up before the book has finished, then I just leave it on the last page it refers to and tear off another envelope corner to use.

I think my Dad would be nodding his approval and my grandchildren would be giving me the approbation of being 'well green, Granny'.

My dad wasn't really a spy

Brenda Ellison

It was 1939. I was a four-year-old girl on a family holiday at Scarborough. Life was blissful. Everyday we went to the outdoor swimming pool. I played beach ball in the shallow pool with other children and then went to swim with my dad in the adult pool. On September 3rd it all stopped and we returned to Newcastle upon Tyne.

Some time later we were going on the bus to Tynemouth to visit my Auntie Winnie and Grandma, when I saw a strange thing like a grey elephant in the sky. Mother said it was a balloon, but we were a family with a sense of humour! (It wasn't till years later that I learnt that it was a barrage balloon.) A visit to Tynemouth usually included a walk on the beach, but now rolls of barbed wire blocked the way. After the war I went to Tynemouth with my friend Pat and we found a mine near some rocks. The area was hastily cordoned off.

The government had predicted that the cities would be a target for German bombing raids and children under five years old were evacuated with their mothers. We went to Hepscott near Morpeth. There I had the excitement of being in the railway signal box watching the signalman moving the levers, and the sound and steam as the train came through. As there were no raids then on the city we returned home to Dad. My friend Pat lived next door and her father put in an air-raid shelter underground in their garden. He made the entrance from the dining room through a trap door with a short ladder. Pat was older than me and she had a great idea. We would put torches, toys, bangles and beads in the shelter and call it Aladdin's cave. We closed the heavy velvet curtains over the windows and the room was very

49

dark. It all ended in tears: Pat's father came home early, went to open the curtains and landed in the shelter.

When the raids did start we went to the cupboard under the stairs where I slept soundly in my siren suit. The planes targeted the shipyard and followed the river, returning over the coast road. Any remaining bombs were dropped as they left. One evening when all seemed quiet, without any air-raid warning a plane came over our street and dropped a bomb on a nearby house. We were having a meal but scrambled under the table as the blast blew the curtains into the room. It was the first time I was scared. I thought a German parachutist was coming to kill us.

the first time I was scared

Many of the local schools were evacuated so I went to Jesmond Towers, a boys' school that took five-year-old girls during the war. The fee was £4/14/6 [£4.73p] per term plus 2/6 [12.5p] for stationery. The prospectus stated 'Adequate Air-raid Shelters are provided'. It was an interesting building and the grounds were fun to explore. I remember sliding down the huge mahogany banisters with my friend Frances and her brother. We landed outside the headmaster's door and were in trouble. When the boys were in the gym the girls practised long jump in the sandpit or stood on a stool to sing or recite. Years later when my mother was sorting some paperwork she tore the prospectus in half 'because you wouldn't want that', but I did want it and so rescued it. I have since read the history of Jesmond Towers. I loved that school; it had such a happy atmosphere.

My next school had a large air-raid shelter in the playground, and as raids on the Tyne increased we spent quite a lot of time there. I was sad if we missed English because Miss Dawson was an inspirational teacher. One day the headmistress stood up from the high table during

50

lunch and said we must be sure to tell our parents that the potato we were given was Diploma not Pom (dried potato).

A local family dealing on the black market became the talk of the area when they hoarded so much tinned food in a bedroom that the floor gave way and the dining room ceiling collapsed.

My wartime treats included condensed milk sandwiches, making cinder and treacle toffee, and taking our sugar ration to a shop on Westgate Road to exchange for sweets. Parcels came from America with parachute silk and swan-shaped floating soap. We went to all the cartoon shows at the Tatler Cinema. Our favourite was Tweetie Pie being stalked by Sylvester. I didn't understand why they switched so quickly to the Pathé newsreels with the haunting images of emaciated prisoners in cages.

My father's friend Ken came from Hull with his girlfriend Stella, who wore a very colourful scarf on her head. I heard later that she was a nurse at Beverley Hospital. She was unable to leave on many consecutive days and nights as, due to heavy bombing, other nurses were unable to get to the hospital. Several patients died. The stress caused her to go bald. Eventually her hair did grow back in tight curls.

The shipyards became a regular target for bombers. My parents were very concerned when Spiller's Flour Mills were on fire for several days

a beacon for the bombers

and nights. They acted as a beacon to the enemy and we saw planes caught in the searchlights. A bomb was dropped on Coleman's Fields near Armstrong Bridge, very close to our house. All the ceilings cracked and had to be replaced. My mother's engagement ring was blown off the bedroom mantelpiece and never found.

The local boys loved to collect shrapnel, and the girls enjoyed exploring the trenches near Reid Park Road. Jumping along the tank traps on the edge of the Town Moor was forbidden. We hid in the secret tunnels at the Jesmond Dene Banqueting Hall, where my friend Pat had her wedding reception many years later. Pat's father was chief chemist at Dampney's, later called British Paints, and their building was hit. We went with him to inspect the open lift-shaft, cracked walls and floors and shattered windows.

When I later read Michael Frayn's book 'Spies', I wondered if some of our neighbours had suspected my dad of being a spy. He was far too young and fit to be at home during the war. He had foreign visitors and they spoke in German and Norwegian. He had petrol for the car, spent the days at the docks and then went out again at night with a book of notes. He understood Morse code and used Pitman's shorthand. Whenever there was a news broadcast we had maps on the table. The truth was that he was a hands-on managing director of a fish import business owned by Mr Wisness, the Norwegian consul. Dad had learnt German at school and had Norwegian lessons at evening classes, with conversation practice at the Norwegian Hotel on Osborne Road, where he acted as book-keeper. As the trade was good he was in a reserve occupation; this was reconsidered at regular intervals throughout the war. When Norway was invaded men were rescued from the sea and brought to Tyne Dock. My father, with assistance from dockers, helped to determine their nationality. There is a link between Norwegian and Geordie words which Germans were unable to make.

too young and fit to be at home

At night he was a special constable with the City Police. He kept his uniform in the landing cupboard, and I was tempted to blow the whistle, but unsure of the consequences! Before leaving he would fling me over his shoulder for a fireman's lift 'up the little wooden hill to bed'. It was such fun for me, but he must have known it could be the last time we saw each other. His notebook starts on Wednesday September 4th 1940 and is a fascinating insight into my father's nightlife and a reason for our super efficient blackout curtains. Once I saw Dad's police-issue gun under his scarf. He took the gun with him on duty and I never saw it again.

a gun under his scarf

There was one frightening incident in the house. I was in the kitchen with my mother and my auntie who had just returned home, and my father was upstairs. Suddenly a very large Norwegian seaman burst into the kitchen. My cat leapt onto the top shelf of the pantry breaking nearly all of my mother's precious china. My father took control of the situation. It transpired that the man had been rescued from the sea and thought he was the only one to be questioned before being issued with a ration book, and that he was being accused of spying for the Germans. After that we always kept the door locked.

My dad was athletic and not aggressive, but he could defend himself. When we were visiting the Norwegian Hotel, a man burst into the rooms of the hotel manager, Mr Pederson, and hauled Dad from the sofa to the floor, where they struggled until the huge guard dog stood over the man. I never found out what the argument was about, but they were concerned that the dog might have frightened me. It hadn't, but the man had. The cook brought a special Norwegian cake for me.

My dad was a gifted pianist who loved music. He went to the lunchtime concerts in the Library after exchanging his books. At Christmas he would sing 'Silent Night' in German. When I heard Placido Domingo singing 'You are my heart's delight' in German, it brought back memories of Dad singing while getting ready for tennis or work.

Did that puzzle our neighbours? I will never know.

I had never seen a lemon before

Jean Wilkinson

At first it was a feeling of loneliness. All the adults were preoccupied with the war. My older brother was at grammar school, and was evacuated within the first few weeks, leaving my mother heart-broken. Everyone expected us to be invaded immediately, but time passed in a lull. My aunt and cousin moved in to escape the London blitz, and I settled down to a childhood war existence.

For rationing I had a 'blue book', and so was entitled to extra sweets and oranges in the summer. I was delegated to stand in queues at local shops for rarer commodities. I remember making Cornish pasties in domestic science lessons, with next to no fat in the pastry.

Our school held auctions to raise money for the war effort. Once a lemon was on show. I had never seen a real lemon, or couldn't remember one, and paid 1s/3d [about 6p] for it.

We had leaded windows, and so didn't need the sticky paper strips applied in patterns to windows to minimise the glass shattering. The wrought iron gates and railings of our house were removed to make planes and ships.

eggs to keep the butcher sweet

54

My father had been through the first World War and was discharged deafened by shelling in the trenches. He was very upset when he couldn't join the Home Guard. He had an allotment which supplied us with lots of fruit and vegetables in the summer. He also had hens there and used the eggs to keep the grocer, butcher and coal merchant sweet.

At the end of the war the Council arranged dancing on the tennis courts. At age 14 I thought this was wonderful.

The German cupboard

Dorothy Connelly

I was one year old when war broke out. My family lived in Oldbury, a town in the Midlands close to both Birmingham and Wolverhampton. As this was considered to be a prime potential target area for German bombing my three elder sisters were evacuated to Edgmond Hall, a large country house on the Shropshire border. My eldest sister, who was about 11 or 12 years old, had to assume responsibility for the younger two. She loved it at Edgmond Hall and said that she was apparently very unhappy about returning home. However, I was too young to go with them and stayed in Oldbury with my parents. At home we had an Anderson shelter in the garden, a hole dug in the ground and covered with a piece of corrugated metal. There were bunk beds and paraffin lamps in the shelter and we used to sleep there at night. Because I was just a tot my Dad fitted an empty cold water tank into the side of the shelter as my cot, which hopefully would have given a bit of protection if we had been hit. I am told that my father always sat on a stool beside the entrance of the shelter with a shovel in his hand, ready to dig us out if the shelter collapsed for any reason.

Building Anderson shelters in back gardens. These were issued free to those earning less than £5 a week; others could buy one for £7

I was never aware of being short of food and my Mom made the most delicious chocolate fudge in a large meat tin and cut it into small squares. God only knew what went into it! I also loved Pom, which was a dried potato mix and there was also a dried egg mix which I thoroughly enjoyed. Our main 'sweeties' consisted of a lemonade flavoured sherbet (rather like sugar in texture) which we ate by dipping a 'twig' (1 think it was made of liquorice) into the sherbet and then sucking the sherbet off the twig. In many ways I was unaware of the war, I think because of the stoic attitude of the adults around me and their determination to carry on as normally as possible. However, as I grew older I went to infant school and can remember sandbagged corridors. I can also remember being told to find four different ways home from school so that any invading Germans couldn't capture all the children.

I also have memories of going to school one morning past a pile of rubble, which the previous day had been a small row of houses. We also used to go around collecting shrapnel from the sides of roads and bomb sites, which we would give to the Air Raid Warden. If we gave him the right one we would get a penny (although I don't recall which were the right ones, nor what he did with the pieces we'd retrieved). We could also get into the Saturday matinée at the cinema for free if we took an empty jar or a bag of newspapers and we were often given an orange in addition to free entry.

We lived in a very long street and once the war ended we held a terrific street party. The street was decorated with bunting and tables loaded with food ran the length of the street. Looking back I marvel at the resourcefulness of the women who managed to fill the tables with food.

One aspect of the war, which is with me today, is the 'German Cupboard'. When an item of food which had previously been scarce became available, my mother would buy two tins - one to use and one for the German Cupboard - to ensure that we had plenty of supplies should the country be invaded. To this day I maintain my own German Cupboard - so I am prepared for any eventuality!

Waiting for Zorro

David Barker

I was seven years old when war broke out. I used to go to Saturday morning cinema at the Heaton Apollo (now the site of a Morrison's store) and I can remember going there and looking forward to seeing the final episode of 'The Mark of Zorro' only to find that it was cancelled. Instead we had to go to school for evacuation registration. I was crying bitterly, but this was disappointment in not being able to see the final part of the adventure rather than the thought of being evacuated. (I had to wait a further 12 years before I eventually got to see the final episode of 'The Mark of Zorro'. I was doing National Service and the camp cinema showed the film that I had missed all those years before).

I was evacuated to West Woodburn. We took the train to Bellingham and from there the bus to West Woodburn. We were taken to the Village Institute where all those villagers who had volunteered to take children were waiting. I and three other lads were billeted with Mr and Mrs Simpson. Home was the old Manse and this was probably the best billet in the village. Mr. Simpson was the Chairman of Bellingham UDC, a Methodist lay preacher, Emergency Food Officer and Billeting Officer and he had a car (but no phone). One of the lads was only there a week until his grandmother came to collect him. During this week he had to sleep across the bottom of our bed. A second lad's (Stewart) mother came to collect him soon after, once she had had her new baby, which left just me and Derek. Stewart and I became lifelong friends. Many years later he was the best man at my wedding.

We settled into a routine of going to the Village Institute in the mornings when we would go for walks and visit places of interest. In this way I learned and discovered a lot about the area. It was on such walks that we visited a nearby castle and, despite being north of Hadrian's Wall, discovered a Roman camp and two Roman forts which they had used for training purposes. We also swam in the river Rede. (Many years later I took my children there, telling them that it was a secret place and we would have it to ourselves, only to find that there were six cars there already and more continued to arrive.) In the afternoons we would attend school for lessons. These included 'writing letters home' which on one occasion resulted in my family receiving a letter from me addressed to 'Dear Friends'.

Sundays were more sober experiences. We would go to Methodist Sunday School in the morning, Church of England in the afternoon and then attend a Methodist evening service. On one occasion Derek and I had found two walking sticks and were playing at fencing when the family returned home. This resulted in a sharp reprimand to us for being so frivolous on the Lord's Day.

When Mr Simpson went preaching anywhere I went with him. Roads were very dark because of the blackout. Once, the car went over into a ditch and we had to get a tractor to tow it out. For the last mile I had to run alongside the car holding the front passenger door handle to ensure Mr Simpson didn't run off the road again.

taking the cow to the bull

We used to help at a nearby farm during haymaking and harvesting the cereals. I can remember the locals all standing to one side as the remaining patch of unharvested corn grew smaller and smaller. They knew that as the area diminished there would be a sudden mass exodus of birds, rabbits and other small mammals fleeing as their habitat was finally demolished. Potato picking was a lucrative opportunity. I got dinner and was paid 2/- [10p] for a day's labour. I also got taken out of school sometimes to help the farmer take his sheep to Bellingham market walking five miles there. My first experience of the 'birds and bees' was when I accompanied a farmer taking a cow to be bulled.

Lord Redesdale owned the land in the surrounding area and when he had been hunting in the vicinity his gamekeepers would leave gifts of fish or hare at the Manse. On one occasion my mother was treated to jugged hare when she came to visit me and this led to my family being convinced that I was living off the fat of the land. This impression was probably reinforced when I took home a duck. I had got some duck eggs and a farmer had loaned a hen to sit on them. Three of them

jugged hare and ducklings

hatched and I cared for the ducklings until the autumn when they were killed.

In 1942 a new boy arrived in the village and I had two or three weeks of bullying and fighting before my mother turned up to take me home.

Despite the war they were carefree days, and after the war I visited Mrs Simpson regularly. The war had given me the opportunity to see and experience things that I would never have done if I'd stayed at home in town.

Life by the shipbuilding yards

June Thexton

The day war broke out, I was in Blackpool on holiday with my parents. We hurried home to Barrow-in-Furness where the adults seemed anxiously on alert expecting the Germans to target our vital steel and shipbuilding industries immediately. Windows were hastily criss-crossed with sticky brown tape, sandbags amassed outside public buildings, and everyone was encouraged to have buckets of sand ready to put out fires. Later, residents were issued with stirrup pumps and had buckets of filthy water standing about -

useful for watering the garden! Large metal tanks of reserve water appeared on street corners for use by fire fighters. Lights at night had to be eliminated with blackouts at windows, streetlights all but extinguished, car headlights shielded, and public transport had weird low blue lights which were further dimmed by the usual heavy pall of cigarette smoke. Winter nights became ominously dark - not that I was ever allowed out on my own, though we still played in the street till the gloom got the better of us.

I began Junior School that autumn and I vaguely recall routines involving what to do when the siren sounded and how to fit our gas masks which we carried everywhere in the regulation cardboard box. When these wore out, people constructed their own individual boxes from Rexine or oilcloth, which lasted better.

my cousin was born in a Morrison cage

Eventually, though still no enemy planes had come our way, precautions were strengthened. Air-raid shelters were built to house families: corrugated iron ones (Andersons) in gardens, brick and concrete ones in back streets to take about twenty, large ones near public buildings. If none of these was appropriate, large metal cages with solid tops called Morrisons were installed in homes. They filled the room so that some people had to sleep in them or eat their meals off them. My cousin was born in one, so my mother informed me later. She was in attendance, there being no handy midwife available.

The neighbourhood children found the new outdoor facilities ideal for setting up camps and dens to play witches and fairies or cowboys and Indians and later, of course, Germans and British. Even today the strange odour of damp concrete takes me immediately back.

When rationing of food began, sweets, alcohol and cigarettes were scarce and provided opportunities for the black market and 'wide boys' to operate. Or so we heard, though I can't recall my family getting involved, probably because my father who worked in the Town Hall was responsible for setting up a Registration Office to issue identity cards and ration books. People seemed resigned to the system which at least ensured fairness and security - no talk of the 'nanny state' then. In fact, official public notices in the press, on radio

and on posters were vital to everyday life, as was the local authorities' response to the emergency following government instructions. My father's job was thus 'reserved' though many of my friends were not so lucky and their fathers were conscripted into the armed forces. More and more men appeared in uniform and army camps sprang up on the edge of town as did prisoner-of-war camps later.

Our wonderful wild beach beyond the shipyards was now enclosed with barbed wire and death's head notices, and my maternal grandmother had to give up her beach hut. This was not the much sought-after, present-day, colourful affair but a fairly tumbledown shack where her extended family spent many happy days. An RAF airstrip appeared nearby, and we truly expected Germans to come in across the heavily-mined beach but there were still no signs of the enemy by land, sea or air in those early days.

Then more portentous wireless messages from the newsreaders, Alvar Liddell, John Snagge and co, became our constant companions - and

a secret pocket in her corset

from the great Churchill himself. Dunkirk had fallen, the allied defences had not held, and the Germans were just across the Channel. (I had only the vaguest idea how far off that was.) Shock, horror in real life. My mother took me aside and said 'Don't worry, I won't let them get you' which I didn't understand at the time. I knew that she had sewn a secret pocket into her corset where she kept essentials if we had to leave town but it was only later that I wondered if she had got hold of some suicide pills to add to her supplies - how, I don't know. My father's boss, the Town Clerk, ex-navy, keen sailor, took time off from work to take his boat to the south coast to rescue troops, so we had a first-hand account of the great exodus from Dunkirk by little boats.

This was a very anxious time for us children too who only partly understood the threat. The frequent trial wailings of the sirens didn't help. I was impressed by our next-door neighbour, a police superintendent, who showed us the firearm he was allowed to have. Because we didn't have a shelter - our gardens weren't suitable - my parents fitted out our understairs cupboard, apparently the safest place in a house, and bought a put-you-up bed for downstairs where we all slept if there was an alert. It was very crowded in the make-do shelter, especially when our other neighbours, who had had their understairs cupboard removed, joined us complete with our canary in its cage. I couldn't leave it unprotected.

Eventually, after all the false alarms, it happened. In May 1941, we

then the bombing began

suffered a prolonged bombing attack and we moved in with my grandmother and my mother's three brothers and their families in her rather battered terraced house with a shelter in the back street. The shelter became home from home while the bombers droned overhead and frequent fires and explosions lit the sky. The extended family kept its spirits up by singing popular songs - *Roll out the barrel, Hang out the washing on the Siegfried Line* etc - telling yarns and jokes, going into the house to make tea. The menfolk, who were Wardens, toured the streets in their tin hats to see everyone was safe, and reported back on the prayers and hymn-singing elsewhere. I was knitting a purple toy duck for my baby cousin who had a huge strange gas mask by her. After the 'all clear' in the morning, local kids took to the streets to add to their shrapnel collections.

On May 9th, the marshalling yard at the back of our house took a direct hit. I'm not sure what the damage was, as I wasn't allowed in, but we

my dolls were spiked with glass

lost a lot of the roof and every room was spoilt with broken glass. My dolls in my room were spiked with the window blown in on them, as I could have been too. All the dolls went out and I never saw them again. At the end of ten nights, most of the town was affected, and in shock. One of my uncles worked with the Rescue Team and was very quiet about what he saw. My father's family Methodist Church was totally destroyed and he never had the heart to go back. Mercifully for us, the bombers decided they'd done enough to ruin our shipyard and its warships and submarines, and turned their attentions to Liverpool again. We had mixed feelings about that.

Obviously, we couldn't return home. I liked living at my Gran's. She was widowed in her forties and had assumed the role of matriarch early on. A strong personality, she ruled her flock - now up to ten of us - with practical 'no weeping and wailing here' commonsense, always ready to offer help to those less fortunate, be they stray animals or frail old ladies. She loved a joke and listened to all the comedy shows on the wireless. I can still hear her wonderful laugh. She made bucketfuls of Scotch broth - not much mutton, a lot of barley - on her very basic gas-cooker to sustain us and, at Christmas, lovely trifle. I still use her recipe.

One of the uncles had an allotment which we all helped with and where we took picnic teas in the summer. He let me grow strawberries in it. So I had to smile when people occasionally pitied me for being an only child. Finding a space for yourself was the problem. To ease that situation, my father

one culture shock...

contacted his country cousins in the Duddon Valley and we moved in with the eldest in his remote cottage near Broughton. A culture shock indeed! They had preserved eggs in the cellar where we were sleeping on the floor, with stored apples and musty hams hanging up, and a dry outside toilet with two holes.

...and another

We didn't stay long, but moved again to the cousin with a modern bungalow nearer the station for Dad to get to work. I went to the village school for a while - another culture shock! There were only three classes: infant, junior, and senior all in one large room with partitions. This was a doddle for me. I didn't learn much except how to cut a hole in a minute piece of cloth, darn it, sew a button on it, and use it as a patch, much to the amazement of my mother who was an expert make-do and mender. Our teacher, an affable rolypoly person, took us on frequent nature walks, where I and my new friend from Manchester helped to push her up the hills.

Come the autumn and the 11+ exams looming, my family decided I must return to civilisation as we knew it. Although I loved my spell in the country, I've never wanted to live there since. Our house was now repaired but we returned to camp out at Grandma's while my parents - mainly Mum - sorted out the interior. There was everything to do but she wouldn't let me help. She didn't let me return till all was to her satisfaction. The stress of all this was getting to all the adults, I think.

Fortunately, despite occasional alerts, no more sustained bombing took place. There was just the odd bomb jettisoned on return flights, or rumours of German airmen parachuting into the woods.

The BBC continued to be our lifeline to what was happening elsewhere. The Home Service, no doubt strictly censored and controlled, took us through the major war zones, now including Asia where one of the uncles was now serving in the RAF in Burma. Two other uncles continued as foremen platers in the yard, working masses of overtime while my father had many late meetings with the Emergency Committee when he wasn't fire-watching on the roof of the Town Hall, a perilous job in the westerly gales that frequently hit our isolated peninsula.

a trip to the dentist was frightening

Shortages of everything remained a problem. We benefited from the daily exhortations of Marguerite Patten on how to produce wonderful meals from dried egg, spam [processed meat], snook [a kind of fish] and other strange ingredients. Once we heard that a shipment of dried fruit had come in from Australia, but after queuing for ages we discovered the packages to be infested with grubs so no Christmas cake after all. The wireless's Family Doctor's avuncular tones kept us on the right track with homely remedies and injunctions to keep fit. GPs still dispensed medicine from their surgeries. A trip to the dentist was truly frightening. All the younger dentists were in the forces and we were left to the tender care of the retired or incompetent. Anaesthetic was non-existent and the road-drill treatment was horrendous. My generation still have teeth but rather knocked-about ones: no orthodontics then.

My entry to the Grammar School in 1943 presented problems. This was a girls' school of the traditional kind and the uniform specification made no concessions. My mother managed to fulfil them by unpicking an old suit of my father's, washing and ironing the good bits, and turning them. Then, using the school's pattern, she constructed the navy tunic which had to be 'just touching the knee at the back when kneeling' and have 'bindings exactly three quarters of an inch wide'. The rest wasn't so arduous except that the required 'ward shoes for indoor wear' were hard to come by and I resented using up my clothing points on them.

Hockey boots were unobtainable so I took to the field in the football boots of one of my relatives and with a second-hand stick. I was never going to be any good at it anyway. We did learn to swim, though, in what remained of the public baths. The pool had been spared but the water remained unheated, while our gym mistress patrolled the edge in her sheepskin assuring us it would be OK when we got in. We had cups of hot Oxo to restore life on coming out.

Most of us went to school on our bikes and the bike sheds were the only bit of the site shared with the adjacent boys' school; otherwise apartheid reigned. Parts of both schools' fields were taken up with large air-raid shelters and the anchorage for a barrage balloon. The heating system, never good at the best of times with open quads to cope with, meant that we sat in lessons in our gabardine macs, scarves and gloves in winter.

Barrage balloon anchored to trucks

We were nevertheless enthusiastic correspondents with 'approved' sections of the forces, mainly sub-mariners on Barrow-built subs and we even knitted socks etc for them, and held sales of work to provide funds for the Red Cross in our break times. In our free time, we were great film fans and went to the pictures when we could afford it to enjoy what Hollywood offered and, less jolly but equally interesting, what Pathé News could show us of current events. Towards the end of the war, the scenes from Buchenwald etc made a lasting horrific impression on us that has never faded.

The last years of the war were less memorable for us once our forces started to make inroads into the enemy. Life was still drab and austere for our parents but we had youthful energy on our side and, when VE Day in 1945 finally came, large groups of family and friends congregated in the main square to celebrate. As the sun went down, all the lights in the surrounding buildings went on, people had lanterns of various kinds, mysteriously there was music and everyone danced and sang, including Gran.

It was over, but the next bit proved pretty demanding too. Even the wonderful fireworks we had on VJ Day could not blank out the news from Hiroshima.

An evacuee comes back

Joan Congleton

Sunday, 3rd September 1939, was warm and sunny, and I remember skipping happily between Mum and Dad, fascinated by our shadows on the pavement. Suddenly the sound of a siren made the summer air ugly, and our shadows were stilled with the shocked realisation that war with Germany had been declared and our lives, like those of millions of others, were to change forever.

Back home Dad was immediately called up, while Mum and I had to learn to cope with life alone and prepare for the birth of her baby, due that December. On my fifth birthday, in October, I started at Cowgate Infant School, Newcastle, from where I was evacuated to Cumberland with hundreds of other children. With our cases, gas masks and labels we kissed goodbye to our crying mothers, then waved forlornly from the moving train.

Many evacuees were lucky with their billets but my friend, Dorothy, and I were not. However, we learnt to adapt and cope with change and hardship. I found solace in the village school where I was allowed to help with the slower learners. So the seeds of desire to become a teacher were sown, and the beauty and fascination of the countryside kindled a lifelong interest. My mother perceived unhappiness, and after about a year Dad came on one of his leaves and brought me home.

At first I felt alienated and estranged from my family. However, there was no time for brooding, for a baby sister was born soon after my seventh birthday. Life was busy, and I sometimes had to take on adult responsibilities in wartime Newcastle. The Anderson shelter in the back garden needed to be checked each day: the blankets aired, food supplies replenished and flasks filled with hot drinks in case we were there for the night, as indeed we often were. We all dreaded the sound of the night siren, being woken out of deep sleep and carried downstairs in our siren suits to the shelter, where we listened for German planes and bombs. Vickers Armstrong's ammunitions factory, the main target, remained unscathed, but

shelter blankets to be aired, flasks to be filled

Manors Goods Station took a battering. In spite of all the disruption, we had to go to school next morning, picking up bits of shrapnel dropped from nocturnal flying shells on our way.

The dominating figure of Police Sergeant Burns was a comforting presence, as he led us across the busy road, or kindly called at our house to check that my mother, on her own with three children, was safe and happy. Sometimes it was to chide her about a chink of light showing through the blackout curtains. Street lights were turned off, but torches were allowed for dark nights. Food was scarce and essentials rationed, with few luxuries, so I made sure I was one of the first in the queue outside the Co-op, often waiting two hours for a plain rice cake. My main concern, however, was how to survive each month on a twelve ounce sweet ration. Gifts of food from the USA and Canada were gratefully received: after a disastrous attempt at an eggless cake my mother was so glad to have powdered egg (I remember the waxed box and the American flag). Shiny red apples and powdered chocolate from Canada were collected in my gas mask tin. The making of chocolate fudge from it was almost as good as the taste.

I think it would be in 1944 that American soldiers ('the Yanks') were billeted in enormous bell tents on a field near Kenton Bar (we now know that it was in preparation for D-Day). We children enjoyed their temporary friendship and generosity, shouting 'Got any gum, chum?' as they passed down the street. Of course they always had. They mingled easily with the local population, who welcomed them into their homes.

Life went on. The cinema was a means of escape from grim realities, and the wireless was the main source of entertainment. It played a large part in informing us what was happening on the Front. When news got around that Mr Churchill was to address the nation, everyone made sure they were at home, and families huddled around the wireless to listen to his inspirational words. The country was united under his leadership, and we never thought for one moment we would lose the war. We pulled together in one tremendous effort as war brought out the best in everyone. Such a pity the same spirit does not exist today.

Dried eggs and dark nights

Ruth Lesser

Two things loom large for me in my memories of the war: dried eggs and dark nights. I can still picture the shelf my father erected over the front door for extra storage in our cramped house. Its main purpose was to house the large tin of dried eggs our prudent Yorkshire mother had obtained as emergency supplies to supplement the rations. It was still there when the war ended. But other tins were stored in the pantry, and we four children were no strangers to meals made from reconstituted dried eggs. They went into cakes, Yorkshire puddings and biscuits, of course, but featured frequently in holes cut in the centres of slices of fried bread. Could it be dried eggs that put me off all cakes for a lifetime except those that are rich with dried fruit (of which we didn't have much during the war)?

We did other makeshift things, too. One was making 'cream' for special occasions out of milk and margarine, with a special pumping jug that someone must have persuaded my mother to buy. We also saved potato peelings and various scraps to be boiled for pigs, as a variant contribution to Digging for Victory. My parents had a soft spot for pigs, as my grandfather used to keep two or three to supplement the family budget. He reportedly disciplined them to stand on a platform to wait for their food: this meant they could be fed on Sundays without his having to change out of his Sunday best. Fortunately rations could be supplemented by visits to British Restaurants, canteen-like institutions where you could get a hot meal cheaply. My father used to walk us children the two miles there, in order to give my mother a break. She had been urged to return to teaching (forbidden to married women before the war, but now essential with many male teachers away) and needed her rest.

tin flowers and parachute bras

Another unusual wartime activity was to collect tins, not for recycling, but to cut with secateurs into shapes of stems and flowers: it seems, extraordinarily enough, that there was a demand for them to raise funds at the church fêtes. I'm not sure the sales were worth the cut fingers. More sensibly we did a lot of knitting for soldiers. For my mother and older sister these were quantities of socks: for me they were squares for blankets. To get enough wool for them we used to unpick old cardigans, wind them into skeins on our thumbs and elbows, and wash them to get the kinks out. My mother and sister were so skilled and committed that they knitted in the cinema, my mother even being able to turn sock heels on the four needles in the flickering dark. We also seemed to be endlessly darning our own socks and stockings on mushroom-shaped holders. It was possible occasionally to get rejected parachutes without clothing coupons. The white silk was lovely, and ideal for petticoats. The camouflage patterned silk was a mixed blessing, especially when made up into bras.

Identity cards were issued, though we did not always carry them, so my father drilled us into remembering our own numbers in case we were confronted. I still recall mine: KBAC2822.

The dark nights, of course, were due to the blackout. My father was a Fire Watcher, which meant that we held the locality's pump and its bucket at our house. We rehearsed with the family racing to refill the bucket. Fortunately it never had to be tested in practice, as it had to be primed, and the hose would have provided a limited reach between bucket and fire. I accompanied my father on his inspections sometimes, mainly because the skies were bright with stars in the absence of street-lights, and he knew the names of the constellations. For me as a child the darkness was not inherently frightening. When I was old enough (about 12, I think) I took over from my

stirrup pump

siblings the pocket-money job of delivering early morning newspapers at some distance from where we lived. This meant getting up at six and walking through the suburban streets on my own in the winter darkness. I don't recall any fear of being alone, even when delivering papers on Cemetery Road or Necropolis Road. Today's parents might have had some concerns, but we felt secure then about strangers we might meet. (Newspapers, cut into squares and on a string loop, had another role in our lives, as toilet paper was in short supply.)

There was one situation where the dark nights did have their fears for me, though. My father's widowed mother had moved to a street parallel to our cul de sac, and I used to spend most nights with her to keep her company. It was connected to our 'grove' by a narrow snicket between the gardens of the houses, and it was always a relief to me to get safely past another incoming snicket. (My fears may have been connected with having seen 'The Wolfman' – a werewolf thriller

- at the cinema, which my mother had assumed to be a nature film). At my grandmother's house there was warmth and light, with the smell of baked teacakes (brown, plain white and lonely currants) always on Thursdays. She let me stay up late, with cereal and warm milk, to listen to *In Town Tonight* 'stopping the roar of London's traffic' on the wireless. I was at my Grandma's the night Bradford had the only bomb dropped on its centre. It fell on Lingard's café, memorable to me as our neighbour was the manageress and my mother used to take us children there for tea as a treat. But I slept soundly through the night of The Bomb, and had the humiliation of being the only one in my class at school who had not shared the excitement. German bombers had unloaded several bombs in the countryside, though, shedding their weight as they returned from bombing the ports and industrial cities in the west. Their craters provided popular venues for Sunday excursions for us and many others.

crater tours

Towards the end of the war we were given nylon stockings once by an American GI cousin of my father. He was based in Germany and came on a sentimental visit to trace relatives in Bradford. As a 14-year-old I was delegated to escort him, and to meet relatives I also didn't know. I was somewhat shaken to find that they assumed I was his wife. I had come across GIs before, when my class from school was sent potato-picking near Beverley in the summer holiday, but I never got close enough to look for nylons.

When the war in Europe ended, VE Day, we children hurried into the centre of Bradford to join the crowds. The squares were tightly packed, people dancing and strangers jubilantly embracing each other. We stuck close together with my brother, in case we got swept away. I remember a puzzled thought I had at that time: that there would be nothing for the newspapers to write about now, as they seemed to me to be entirely filled with the progress of the war. But I was wrong.

Back to a requisitioned house

Vyvian Fryer

O n a beautiful sunny day in 1939 I remember sitting with my parents and 15 year-old sister beside our large radiogram. I was not quite six years old, and it is one of my earliest memories. Faces were grave. I was aware of a man making a lengthy speech. The last sentence is engraved on my mind: 'This country is at war with Germany'. That's the end of the memory, but there must have been consternation all round, particularly as my father had served in the army throughout World War One.

At this time we were living in Whitley Bay, but my family belonged to Bradford and had only moved north for work reasons shortly before my birth.

As far as I can recall, normal life changed quickly after that. My mother took my sister and me, along with most of the family furniture (some was stored), to live in a rented house in Bradford near her family. My father had to remain, and moved into the house of close friends, leaving our house empty. Throughout the war, in addition to his normal occupation, he served with the Royal Observer Corps. We spent about three years in Bradford. We visited local cinemas at least once a fortnight, as the main available entertainment. Films changed two or three times a week. I remember only one air raid – an incendiary bomb on the city centre, which looked spectacular from our attic window. My sister had been close to School Certificate, and had to sit it there amongst strangers. For a while she did office work, but upon being 'called up' became a nurse.

We returned to Whitley Bay in 1943. It was sad to observe our home, one of a pair of semis requisitioned by the RAF. When they moved out it was in a terrible state, and it took a while to get it put right. Due to bombing the staircase window had gone and was boarded up, making the hall very dark. The house is on the front of the north end of Whitley Bay. On what is now a miniature golf course there was an 'Assault Course' which, when not in use, made a wonderful playing area for us children (at least parts of it). The promenade above the beach was a no-go area due to extensive barbed wire.

I remember the excitement when VE Day came, but don't recall any special parties. Being too young to understand about rationing, I am amazed in retrospect that I always had a party with a special tea when my birthday came round.

My family were aliens

Michael Cullen

I was born in 1942, so my memories of the war are based on discussions with my elder sister. My father went to America in the 1920s to look for work. He came back in 1926 when he got engaged to my mother. He returned to America followed by my mother and they were married in New York on 26 October. Consequently when my older siblings were born they were American citizens. When the recession hit America my father was out of work and my mother and her four children returned to England in 1938. She campaigned for my father, who had taken American citizenship, to be allowed to return too. He eventually sailed back from New York on 3 September 1939, the five-day crossing taking two weeks as the ship zig-zagged across the Atlantic to avoid attack by the Germans.

As American citizens my family were classed as aliens and so they were questioned by the Security Services and had regular visits from them until America joined the Allies later in the war. Initially my mother, sister and three brothers were evacuated. They were supposed to go to Ambleside but due to a bureaucratic error found themselves in Amble. They only stayed two months before returning home.

My family lived in High Heaton and one of the first bombs to fall on Newcastle fell in our back garden leaving a huge crater. The garden was never the same again. Fortunately as the sirens hadn't gone off my family were still in bed rather than in the air-raid shelter in the garden, although a passing cyclist was killed. There were also people killed at the school caretaker's house on Newton Road. The bomb caused cracks in our walls and the windows were blown out, but we received a visit from the Lord Mayor as one of the first families affected by the bombing.

One Sunday morning my mother was going to Mass and she can recall seeing a dog-fight between planes going on above her. She was so terrified that she knocked on someone's door to let her in. On another occasion my sister was with my father at the Lyric cinema, now The People's Theatre, when there was an announcement that bombers were approaching. As she left the cinema to go to the shelter the anti-aircraft guns were going, which made it very frightening. That night St Gabriel's vicarage, which was close by, was bombed.

Groceries were rationed and my mother registered with both the Co-op and the Hadrian Supply Company, dividing the family's ration allowance between them. This meant that if one store didn't have what she needed she might be able to obtain it at the other store. One day she left me in my pram outside and must have been queuing for some time, as when she came out I had eaten nearly a whole loaf of bread which had been intended to feed the entire family.

When America joined the war some of their troops were stationed at Debden Gardens, near Benfield. They used the garage on the corner of Stephenson Road and Chillingham Road for their motor pool. My brother and his friends used to go there and, as the Americans didn't have rationing, the soldiers would give them tins of pineapple, a very welcome treat. However my only clear memory of the war is of being taken down into the air raid shelter after the war, which is ironic considering that, had my family been in the shelter the night the bomb fell, I wouldn't be here to tell the tale.

Life on the edge of an aerodrome

Jacqui Cryer

I shall always remember 'the day war broke out', as Rob Wilton, a comedian of the forties, used to say. I had been given the money to go to the Nestlé chocolate machine outside the local grocery shop. When I returned with my red bar of chocolate I was told that we were at war. I was seven years old at the time and I can remember in my mind planes crashing and noise. I can only think that I must have seen pictures in the papers of what was happening in

Poland. Those first few nights in September were like daylight: there were clear skies and a full harvest moon.

Where I lived in Doncaster was at the edge of an aerodrome and I can remember being out in the garden with my father talking to the airmen who were patrolling the perimeter. The aerodrome was mostly for civil aircraft. I recall the KLM Handley Page HP42s bringing passengers to the St Leger race meeting, which was across the road from the aerodrome[3]. In those days there were no concrete runways, only grass.

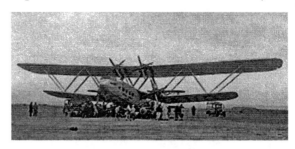

Handley Page HP42

with passengers waiting under the wings

As the war progressed we had Wellington bombers stationed there. We used to count them out and count them coming back. We saw crash landings as damaged planes tried to land safely. I can remember one not being able to stop and doing a nose drive into a farmyard.

We got to know the airmen and had them over for Sunday lunch. We had one called Frank Pinder from Sheffield who always got the job of slicing the beans. I have never been able to match his skill. Then he stopped coming.

I remember after Dunkirk going up the road to the bus stop and seeing men lying on stretchers on the pavement. Later we discovered

---

[3] *Editor's note: These civilian planes were impressed into the Royal Air Force for service at the outbreak of the war, but by 1940 all of them had been lost.*

that, as Doncaster was on the main LNER railway, the wounded had just been put on trains to get them away from the south coast as soon as possible. They were billeted in wooden huts on the aerodrome and I took books and newspapers to them. In those days there was no barbed wire fencing and no such thing as security guards.

On the racecourse they built a prisoner-of-war camp mostly for interned Italians who had businesses in England in September 1939. There were no Great Escapes from that camp; they were better off here.

Wellington bomber (or 'Flying Cigar')

We were issued with an Anderson shelter, which Dad erected in the ground under the hedge that divided the garden from the aerodrome in the hope that it would be hidden. We were provided with four bunk beds and we had a paraffin stove. We kept a small supply of food in the shelter. There were quite a few air raids because of the big railway works at Doncaster and also the nearness of the steel works in Sheffield and Rotherham. Any bombs left over seemed destined for us.

I was now in junior school but our building had been taken over by the army as temporary billets as it was a single storey building. We were re-housed in the old Infirmary in the town centre. It was a segregated school so we girls took it in turns with the boys for the mornings and afternoons. It was an ancient building with stone spiral staircases that I was frightened of falling down. If there had been an air raid and the All Clear did not go until 3 am we did not go to school in the morning. So you can imagine what we felt like as the clock neared the deadline.

When the war first started we were all encouraged to Dig for Victory. Our garden soil was very sandy and whatever was planted was eaten by rabbits that came from the aerodrome so my gran decided to keep chickens. My father was away most of the time building factories and hospitals and my Mum hated worms so it seemed the best solution. Eggs were rationed so if anyone registered with you for eggs you got an extra allowance of meal. This was OK whilst the chickens were laying but there was always a time when they were not. We used to preserve eggs in isinglass. When we stopped getting white flour my gran sifted flour through georgette to remove the bran which, mixed with potato peelings, was the chickens' stable diet. We had one large white cockerel called Paddy who met his fate come Christmas.

Over the next months and then years people adapted to the rationing. At Christmas we got a few extra coupons for sweets. Everyone shared knowledge of what was available; it was a treat to buy a bag of broken biscuits without coupons. There was a great camaraderie among the communities.

Clothing coupons were the worst when you grew quickly and had to wear strict uniform at high school even down to dark green knickers, which doubled up as PE kit. Even when I left school in 1948 my dreaded gymslip was made into a skirt and blouses dyed.

I think my worst experience of the war was the day outing to Bridlington. My mum and a friend decided to take my friend and me for the day to the seaside. It did not start well. There had been a raid during the night and when we got to town Station Road was closed

the stick of bombs missed the train

81

because of an unexploded bomb. We had to make a detour. We got to Bridlington fine and went on the beach that had barbed wire across only allowing a small access. During the course of the day we saw a German fighter being chased out to sea by a Spitfire. After a while the Spitfire returned but according to Mum he had not shot it down or he would have done the victory roll on crossing the coastline.

On our return a German bomber had followed our train and launched a stick of bombs at Beverley fortunately missing the train. We had to change trains at Hull. Someone's rifle went off. Looking outside the station all that could be seen was flattened buildings except for the church. We never took any more day trips to the coast.

The end of hostilities was memorable. A few weeks after the war in Europe ended we went to London for a holiday. We were in Whitehall. There was a buzz of expectancy in the air so we went to Fleet Street to find out. The war in the Far East was over. The city went mad dancing in the streets, especially service personnel. People climbed lampposts to get better views. Later in the day the crowds converged on the Palace where the King, Queen and the two Princesses in evening dress and tiaras came on the balcony. More singing and dancing.

At last there was something really great to celebrate. Now we could look forward to the better future promised by the politicians.

What is surprising is how many memories we have kept for seventy years.

'Missing presumed dead'

Margaret Isobel Armstrong

I played happily in the garden of our semi-detached house oblivious to the world around me, except that I had all my dollies' washing to peg out before the sun disappeared. What on earth was that terrible noise, or rather sound, penetrating my ear-drums? Mam and I rushed through the garage towards the front of the house. The terrified pitch of that sound slowly came nearer and nearer. I could see my maternal Grandmother running as if in a drunken stupor towards Mam and me. I suddenly realised the pitiful sound was coming from her. She was sobbing and could hardly stand. At once we took hold of her and brought her indoors. 'Margaret, go and play with your dollies and be quiet, your Grandmother is not well'. I reluctantly left the scene but somehow was drawn back so I hid behind the half-open dining-room door. 'Oh Peg,' said Grandmother, who was still sobbing and waving a paper about. Mam grasped the rather ordinary looking paper. She immediately sank on to the sofa next to Grandmother, putting her arm around her old Mother's shoulders. I strained to hear what they were saying: 'missing presumed dead'. What did it mean?

Opening the door to its full width I decided to confront them. Although I was just over four years old I knew that something terrible had happened. 'Come in, Banjo', said Mam (Banjo was my nickname given to me by Dad as I was always entertaining and pretending to strum an instrument). I sat down quietly nearby. Mam read the telegram again as if she disbelieved the message.

Grandmother had two sons, Robert aged 29 and James aged 19, as well as Mam. Both brothers were serving in the Royal Navy and by chance both were on board the same ship, HMS The Prince of Wales. President Roosevelt and Winston Churchill had secret meetings on board discussing tactics (see p 4) and somehow the Japanese had

HMS The Prince of Wales

learnt of this and sent submarines to destroy the ship and other vessels of the Fleet. The very important leaders had long gone when torpedoes struck the ship and she was so badly damaged that she sank, taking many of the young souls with her. Robert and James could not be accounted for, and therefore were presumed dead.

The whole house seemed to sense the tragedy. I rushed upstairs to my bedroom to find my signet ring made by my Dad. He was in the Fleet Air Arm and was far away. The ring he made me was so beautiful. It was carefully styled in Perspex from an aeroplane windscreen and set inside was a gold heart. I clutched the little ring and wished very hard indeed that Dad, Uncle Robert and Uncle James would come home safely.

In fact, Robert was captured by the Japanese and was kept in a dreadful prison camp in Sumatra for three years. He was liberated by the Australians and eventually came home safely. James, the younger brother, escaped on a raft and was picked up by an Australian vessel and is still alive to this day at the ripe old age of 87 years. Someone was indeed looking after them, thank God.

Brother evacuees

Pat Murray

Two days before the start of the war, at the age of seven I found myself in a queue outside Gateshead station waiting for a train to take us to Guisborough. From there we were transported to the vicarage at Wilton where we were allocated to the homes where we would be staying. My two elder brothers were staying at a farm whilst I and Billy (a 13 year old boy) were to stay with a gamekeeper's family. Their house was isolated and some three miles from the school at Lackenby. We used to get up at seven, have breakfast and then set out at about eight to walk there. Luckily, after a few mornings we noticed a milk float going our way and the driver was kind enough to drop us off near the school. As the school had to cater for both local children and evacuees, it entailed three of the classes being taught simultaneously in the big hall. As I had an early breakfast I used to eat half of my sandwiches at morning playtime.

At weekends we always started Sunday dinner with a large Yorkshire pudding smothered in gravy. The gamekeeper had a motor bike and sidecar and would take us out for a ride.

he had to start work at 14

By Christmas my eldest brother was 14 and returned to Gateshead as he now had to start work. My other brother, Jimmy, and I were moved to Lackenby which consisted of two rows of houses, probably about 60 in all. At one end of the houses was a playing field and at the other a farm. Jimmy was in a different row of houses from me but we shared a shilling [5p] Postal Order which my Mother sent each week. Out of my 6d [2½p] the man of the house where I stayed, who was unemployed, used to take 2½d [1p] to buy himself a single packet of Woodbines [cigarettes].

On Saturdays we would go to the pictures at Normanby. Whilst there we would sing *We're going to hang out our washing on the Siegfried Line*. The 'cheeky' (attendant) used to march up and down with his stick to make sure we were all singing patriotically.

In February 1940 my sister took us back to Gateshead. At first All Saints School was closed due to the shortage of teachers. I was taught in a small group in a house on Windmill Hills, then in small classes in the GYMS rooms where Tesco's is now, until an air raid shelter was built in the school playground. At the top of my street Anderson shelters were provided and we furnished ours with bunk beds for when there was an air raid, generally at night. In contrast my aunts, who lived in the next street, had an air raid shelter of brick in their back yard, which they shared with their downstairs neighbours. Off the High Street there was a public air raid shelter. My eldest brother, Harry, who was now 17, was an ARP Warden and was provided with a tin hat, a bucket of sand and a stirrup pump.

Signs of military activity included a small troop of soldiers billeted in a disused school opposite us. On the Windmill Hills there was a small detachment of the RAF whose job was to put a barrage balloon in the air to dissuade Nazi bombers. If there was an air raid my friends and I would look for shrapnel the next morning. The most serious air raids near us were at Manors and Spiller's (the only one I remember happening during the day).

Food was rationed but my Mother always seemed to have butter with her meals. If a certain type of food became available, word spread like wildfire and a queue would form at that shop, such as bananas at Sampson's. Sweets were rationed but I used to have a little extra as my Aunt Nora had a sweet shop and my sister, Betty, brought some when she was on leave from the NAAFI.

Occasionally at school we were given blended cocoa, a form of drinking chocolate provided by our Canadian friends.

Comics were in short supply but as I had a weekly order for the boys' comics *Adventure, Wizard, Hotspur* and *Rover* I was able to read them and sell them on.

Royal Navy missions in the Med

Mark Johnson

In 1944, at the age of seventeen, I volunteered for service in the Royal Navy. This was a year before the war ended. All males were conscripted at age eighteen, but volunteers got their choice of which service to join. All naval shore bases have an 'HMS' title, although they are sited on land. My first training took place at HMS Royal Arthur at Skegness (now a Butlin's holiday camp). My second was specialist training at HMS Ceres at Wetherby in the Naval Supply and Secretarial School (now an open prison for young offenders). I then went on to the naval depot HMS Pembroke at Chatham to await posting overseas.

HMS St Brides Bay

When this arrived, it was to a Bay class frigate in the Mediterranean Fleet. I had a long journey to reach it. I took passage from Woolwich dockyard on an aircraft carrier, HMS Fencer, arriving at Malta a few days later. My ship, HMS St Brides Bay, had already left for Alexandria. So I then took passage on a cruiser, HMS Newcastle, to Alexandria, but HMS St Brides Bay had already left for Port Said! To speed things up the Naval RTO (Rail Transport Officer) stuck me on a train from Alexandria to Port Said. I was tired and weary, having been encumbered with a kit bag and hammock throughout my journeys. The supply rating whom I relieved was pleased to see me. His father had died and he was on compassionate release, so as to take over his father's business which was essential to the war effort.

First mission

The war in Europe ended quickly not long after that, but the war against Japan still continued for a further four months until atom bombs brought it to a conclusion. My first mission involved me with service beyond the Mediterranean Sea. Prior to World War Two the Royal Navy had a base in Shanghai. They used specially adapted river gunboats to patrol the River Yang Tse to prevent Chinese pirates from attacking merchant shipping. Three of these gunboats, HMSs Aphis, Cockchafer and Scarab, were deployed in the Mediterranean during World War Two. They were used to bombard Rommel and his Africa Korps, as they retreated through Egypt and Libya. HMS St

escorting gunboats on their way to China

Bride's Bay was despatched to Tobruk harbour to collect these gunboats and take them halfway back to their Chinese base. We escorted them along the North African coast, calling at Alexandria and Port Said, through the Suez Canal, more calls at Port Sudan and Massawa (Eritrea), and finally arrived at Aden. A Pacific Fleet destroyer took over guardship duties for the remaining travel to Shanghai. This base and patrols continued until 1949. Tragically another gunboat, HMS Amethyst, got in between the army of Chairman Mao (communist) and Chiang Kai Shek (nationalist). The Red Army shelled the Amethyst, and twenty men were killed and forty wounded. Though badly damaged the Amethyst limped back to Shanghai. That was the end of Royal Navy patrols of the Yang Tse. More than fifty years later I was working on the National Census, and called on an old gentleman in Fenham. He mentioned that he had served in the Royal Navy but said: 'You will not have heard of my ship. It was a gunboat in the Med'. He was amazed when I said: 'Was it the Aphis, Scarab or Cockchafer?'. It was the Aphis, and I told him it did four years patrol on the Yang Tse until Chairman Mao kicked us out of China, and they were scrapped.

Second and third missions

My next mission was patrolling the Palestinian coast to intercept illegal Jewish immigrant ships. On interception we escorted them to Larnaca in Cyprus. On my third mission my ship was acting as duty warship at Gibraltar. Across the Straits of Gibraltar in the international part of Tangier, strikes were going on. We took on board a hundred soldiers of the Manchester regiment, which was then part of the Gibraltar garrison. When we reached Tangier, landing parties quickly stopped the riots and damage. This was 1946, and we were equipped with 1917 Lee Enfield rifles! There were protests from the Soviet Union to the United Nations at this naval and army action in Tangier.

Fourth mission

The Corfu Channel between the Greek island and Albania at one point is only two miles wide. This means that the waters are not territorial, and it is recognised as an international waterway. This was disputed, however, by Albania and its communist leader, Hoxha. They got hold of fifty German mines left over from the war and mined the Corfu Channel. Two British destroyers, HMS Saumarez and HMS Volace, were caught by the mines, with a loss of life of forty men and eighty wounded. We were despatched post haste to the scene as escort to three minesweepers. We took on board Admiral Sir Algernon Willis, who was Commander of the Mediterranean Fleet. This meant that, for a short period, we became the Flagship of the then vast Mediterranean Fleet. An Albanian gunboat tried to harass our minesweepers, but a shot across its bows resulted in a hasty retreat. The Albanian shore batteries were aimed at us: our guns were aimed at them. They thought better of it. The mines were all safely destroyed. Our dead were all buried in the military cemetery on Corfu.

Fifth and sixth missions

The American destroyers USN Edward G Small and USN Power were based at Trieste and Venice, and with them we patrolled the Adriatic. We were protecting Italian trawlers from Tito's partisans. The war was over, but they still regarded Italy as their enemy. We made one little side trip to Pola to disable two German midget submarines in the harbour there. Italy finally ceded Pola to Yugoslavia. It is now in Slovenia and is known as Pula.

On my sixth mission we were despatched to Piraeus in Greece, the port of Athens. Our role here was to patrol the Greek coast whilst the Greek royalists and the British army fought the Greek communist party. The communists lost. We were sent to assist a British troopship, ss Gradisca, which had struck rocks at Gavdos Island off Crete. All the army personnel were safely transferred to an aircraft carrier, HMS Ocean. Then it was back to Malta, where the grand tour had started. We said goodbye to HMS St Brides Bay, and took Italian transport (it was ss Argentinia) from Malta to Toulon. A tortuous 24-hour journey followed on a slow troop train the length of France from Toulon to Calais. The cross-channel ferry then took us to Dover. It was bitter cold in the winter of February 1947. Demob was a few weeks later, and we called for the allocation of our civilian clothing at Fulford Army Barracks in York.

I would not have missed this part of my life as a 17 to 20 year old for a king's ransom.

War on the docks

Donald Davis

In January 1933 my mother and father moved into 8 Wilton Avenue, Walker. They were the first occupants of this brand new house in a brand new estate, designed ahead of its time even by today's standards. In the April of that year I was born but regrettably within four short years my father, an engineer at Parsons, died of pneumonia, leaving my mother to go it alone in early pregnancy with my brother. Times were hard indeed but ironically the forthcoming war would be what you might call her salvation.

Within two years World War Two was upon us and Mum, me and brother William aged two were evacuated to Gainford near Darlington. I was billeted away from them and none too happy. My 'surrogate' mother was a bit short on patience and long on arm reach. I got blamed for much that was the irresponsibility of her two sons, both about my own age. So I spent a lot of time with my mother at her accommodation at the house and surgery of Dr Mawson, the local GP. Mrs Mawson was an absolute gem whom we, a rather bedraggled family, came to rely upon. Food rationing was strict. Dairy products were hard to come by, but we never went without. Mrs Mawson had a chicken farm and my mum was employed by her to pluck and dress chickens ready for the table. Chickens contain eggs, even dead chickens, and so we had copious amounts of unborn shell-less eggs brim full of protein. We had a wonderful time in Gainford. The war was far away in some other place. Although I have travelled this country far and wide I have always avoided Gainford. In my day it was a tranquil village with its village green, blacksmith's forge, grocer and post office. I'll just remember it as it was, through the eyes of a boy of seven.

Returning to Walker some months later, life was hectic, with air raids most nights. Mum became a Fire Watcher, going out with her torch and funny steel helmet looking for incendiary bombs. Grown-ups talked about gas attacks that killed everyone. This frightened me quite a bit. Mum was adamant that we would not go into the Anderson shelter in the garden. 'Get your death of cold in there' she would exclaim; 'when the bombers come we'll sit under the stairs, we'll be OK there'. So nightly we sat or slept under the stairs and through the kitchen window watched the German aircraft making their bombing run right over our house to the River Tyne stuffed with warships only a mile away. On the way to school we would collect bits of shrapnel, some still warm, and swap them with friends. A good piece might get you a couple of newish comics. A bullet case: oh my, you were King and could demand your own price. Our teacher at Welbeck Road insisted that if a raid started whilst we were on our way to school we were to lie down under a hedge till the All Clear.

The Tyne was full of shipping of course, mostly painted grey, being built or repaired. HMS Kelly was an unlucky ship, in and out of Hawthorn Lesleys so many times for damage repairs. One day she just didn't come back. I missed seeing her moored alongside the Hebburn ferry landing when I went to visit Grandma. Lord Louis Mountbatten was the First Officer on the Kelly. He survived the war only to be killed in another war in 1972. He and some of his family were killed when an IRA bomb exploded in their private yacht moored in Sligo harbour, Co Donegal.

Another ship built on the Tyne was going to change my life forever. HMS Victorious, an aircraft carrier, was nearing completion at Vickers Naval Dockyard and already her crew were arriving prior to commissioning. One of those sailors was going to be my future father. Many families in Walker and Wallsend who had room to spare in their homes were obliged by law to accommodate RN personnel. A

HMS Victorious
Corsairs on the flight deck had their wings folded

Billeting Officer would oversee this and deal with any complaints, friction etc. Thus we had a succession of young ratings living with us, looked after by a more senior rating. Chief Petty Officer Jim Gardner from the Victorious was one such supervisor, a nice man, so nice in fact that he and my mum hit it off, and remained together for the next 65 years.

It was about then that I was evacuated once again but this time on my own. I went to Workington in Cumbria. The journey was daunting and with no mum I remember being very sad. It got no better at Workington station, where we formed a line along the platform, clutching our worldly chattels, and were inspected by potential guardians. Gradually the long line dwindled until only me and a few others were left standing. I thought 'What if I'm not picked, maybe they'll send me back home'. Not to be; my luck was about to change. Mr and Mrs Rumford (Auntie Belle and Uncle Bob) came to the rescue. 'Perhaps you would like to come home with us' I think she said, taking my hand, and that was that. I had a wonderful time with them. They were comfortably off with a car and a caravan on a private site near Maryport where we spent many long weekends and holidays. Additionally they loved walking in the Lake District. As a wee boy I was not too enamoured of this pastime but something must have stuck because I have loved the hills ever since. Rock climbing, potholing and anything else you can do on a mountain was just fine by me. I spent about a year with them and I kept in touch with Auntie Belle right up to the mid1980s when she sadly passed away.

There had been very little 'War' in Workington. I think the odd bomb ditched whilst fleeing Glasgow was all the German Air Force could muster. But back on the Tyne it was bad and people suffered nightly air raids with many aircraft. The Luftwaffe were hell bent on sinking the warships moored or being built at Vickers, Palmers, Swan Hunters, Tyne Dock and Hawthorn Lesleys. My (by now) step-dad's ship HMS Victorious was miraculously spared, although often straddled with unexploded bombs.

94

Before Dad's ship eventually sailed, he persuaded Mum to move to his home town, Sale, in Cheshire where he thought we would be safe from the bombing. The journey by rail to Manchester was horrendous: long hours sitting and waiting usually with a blacked-out train overcrowded with troops travelling who knows where. There were interminable stops for air raids or air raid debris. How Mum managed with me and a small baby and all the luggage I do not know, but she did have help from all those bored soldiers standing around with nothing to do but smoke. During the next four years I only saw my new dad fleetingly when he was in some port or other and managed to get a 48 hours pass.

Sale was a pleasant town more or less unbombed with rarely a German plane in sight. One sad moment for me was when I awoke to the drone of a Lancaster bomber circling overhead. I knew that sound, living as I did in the flight path of Bomber Command's RAF Ringway (now Manchester Airport). But this plane was in trouble, the engines 'hunting' and sporadic. The pilot had found the Bridgewater Canal, like a motorway to home, but he didn't get there. As it passed low over our house I could see in the moonlight the damage to her wings. She crashed two miles away in an allotment in Brooklands and all her (New Zealand) crew perished. I went along to the crash site the next morning and even to me, a very little lad, it was such a sad experience. The meaning of war came to me clearly indeed that day. People got killed.

A concluding incident put *finis* to my war but it was not until the early 1970's. Now in the Royal Air Force, I was taking a short break from that other war in Northern Ireland and, on entering Stranraer Lough on the Larne Ferry, I saw HMS Victorious for the last time. She was being scrapped and already down to her waterline. Oh dear, the end to so many childhood memories! I saw her built and I saw her scrapped. She had taken part in every theatre of World War Two: the mid-winter Russian convoys, the Atlantic Ocean chases, the sinking of the Bismark, the Malta convoys with such heavy losses, and finally to the Pacific fighting the Japanese. What a record and what a fine ship! It was the end of a chapter in my life. I was a little sad that day.

The other side of the North Sea

Christa Clemmetsen

After my arrival in 1938 my parents decided to move from central Hamburg to the outskirts of town, about eight miles out. This proved to be a wise decision as we had a very large garden in which my parents used to grow many varieties of fruit and vegetables, so we never had to go hungry. My father was almost 60, which meant that he was not in the army but still worked.

Some events are clearly sketched in my mind. Our house had a cellar and my father had built a bunk bed in it I could lie down during air raids. I remember being carried downstairs, along the narrow stairs to the cellar, past jars of bottled fruit and jam, then lying on the top bunk, watching my parents knit and mend. The year 1943 saw the heavy bombing of Hamburg. It was a glorious summer and the planes came day and night. My mother kept calling from the cellar for us to come down, but my father and I stood at the back door and watched the squadrons against the clear blue sky although I had no idea of the significance. Most likely I did not see the connection either, when we removed the blackout curtains one morning and it remained dark, although we could see the sun through the pall of smoke. Clouds of smoke had drifted across to our suburb. It was very exciting to me when we found whole but singed books that had landed in our garden, carried there by the firestorm. Later that day friends arrived who had lost their houses in town. One poignant vision I still have is that of an older man who came with a very small suitcase. When he unpacked it contained nothing really useful, just some odd socks, a few hankies and some photographs. On the first of these days nine people were in the house when I was put to bed and by morning there were 16. I do remember these numbers but not how long they stayed with us.

My mother used to go to a local hall one or two days a week where women mended soldiers' uniforms. I remember my mother coming home in tears one day, saying that she did not think the war could last much longer, as now everything they were given had already been darned and patched before. Friendships she formed at that time lasted to the end of her life.

The following events must have happened near the end or after the war. We would walk about an hour towards a railway line and people could be seen collecting odd bits of coal that had come off the wagons of passing trains. Much more organised was the gleaning of fields. As we lived right at the edge of town, there were farms in the area. I don't know how the townspeople found out, but news got round that farmer X would open his potato field on Friday at 3 pm. By this time they had ploughed the potatoes up, had people collect all visible potatoes and it was only then that the field was free for the gleaners. People came with little hoes, everyone lined up at the bottom of the field and you hoed and raked all the way to the top, looking for any left-over potatoes.

One black market memory: an elderly cousin of my father's came to visit us from town. She was very excited as she had managed to buy a pound of coffee beans from a man hiding in a doorway. She gave it to my mother but when they opened the brown packet it only contained roasted peas.

At one point all women and children were to be evacuated. We had to get on a train and I remember it being very crowded and hot. Progress was very slow and the train often stopped. After about four hours we arrived in Lübeck (less than one hour normally). As it was already evening my mother decided to get off the train and call on a cousin. At her house we met a visitor who had come from Hamburg by car and was going back the next day. We got a lift home and nobody made us leave after that. My friend down the road had ended up in Bavaria and it was over a year before they returned.

Another vivid memory is the end of the war. Everyone was outside, again in glorious sunshine, when we heard an unearthly noise in the distance. This turned out to be a Scottish regiment, wearing kilts and playing the bag-pipes.

Refugees from Prague

Robert Weiner

We (my Dad, Mum and I) arrived in Britain on 1st June 1939, Jewish refugees from Prague. Mum had taught English so language was no problem for her, but neither Dad nor I spoke a word. We both picked it up fairly quickly but Dad did have some interesting variations (he washed up the crocks in a 'bowel' and reported that I would be arriving in the 'couch' from London). I cannot remember learning English myself and must have simply picked it up from other children as I went along.

Robert with his mother and grandparents in Wenceslas Square: 1935

For the first three months we lived in London but then on 1ˢᵗ September the Germans invaded Poland and war looked inevitable. That afternoon a friend (another Czech refugee) rang to say that he had hired a cab to drive his wife and baby son to Truro and as there were two spare seats, would my Mum and I like to go along? We accepted and so spent the first night of the blackout being driven to the South West of England – a journey to be remembered! By 6 am we had got as far as Torquay, by which time Mum was very unwell with what turned out to be a kidney infection. Dad, who was a doctor, was sent for and within a few days of treatment with M & B (no antibiotics then) Mum was well again. When they came to look around Torquay they could see no reason for moving on to Truro and that is how we came to spend the whole of the War in the Torbay area.

As we were 'friendly aliens' the authorities had little interest in us (unlike Jewish refugees from Germany and Austria, who were 'enemy aliens' and spent some time early on in the war behind barbed wire on the Isle of Man). So we had complete freedom of movement and during our six plus years there we had five different addresses. Renting was very difficult because, of course, there were many evacuees from the various industrial cities and I know Mum spent days and days house hunting.

Initially my Dad was not permitted to work and we lived off charity. Fortunately the regulations gradually changed. First he was allowed to take up work as a science teacher in a boarding school in Crediton and eventually, when he was permitted to resume medical work, he joined the RAMC (Royal Army Medical Corps). Consequently, like so many other children, I spent most of the war without a Dad.

Robert and his parents in 1945 on the Torquay Sea Front

Torbay saw very little enemy action but did experience the American invasion just prior to D-Day. To us boys, rationed to minimal amounts of sweets and chocolate, the American service men were wonderfully generous with their gifts of 'Lifesavers' and chewing gum.

D-Day itself was very memorable. On 5th June 1944 the bay was full of warships and then suddenly, overnight, they and all the Americans were gone. During that night we had an air raid warning and Mum and I spent the whole night in our Morrison shelter. Although, as far as I remember, all was quiet outside, we wondered what was causing the strange earth tremors that we could feel. The explanation came the next morning when it became clear that the landings had taken place on the French coast immediately across the English Channel.

Finally, like everyone else, I have my 'first bananas after the war' story. These came with my Dad's return from West Africa, where he had been posted by the RAMC. It was great to have him back and the bananas were just the icing on the cake.

The view from Normandy

Brian Cryer

On a recent visit to France I was standing on a headland overlooking the Normandy Landing Beaches when my thoughts went back to the morning 65 years ago when we were all assembled in the school hall to hear the news of the Normandy Invasion. I then thought of a similar French schoolboy who could have been living near to where I was standing, and what his thoughts of that morning would be. Perhaps he would have been woken in the early hours by the drone of low flying planes, appearing to be in twos with the second plane having no engine.

Both had three white stripes on their wings and body. All was then quiet and sleep called again. At 6.30 am without warning a deafening barrage of shells landed all around, and when I peeped through the curtains, ships filled the horizon in both directions with flashes as their guns fired. At 7 am the pounding stopped and was replaced by the sound of smaller boats much nearer, accompanied by the blare of gunfire, both big bangs and smaller ra-ta-tat fire. Under our big table seemed the best place. Suddenly the end of the house fell down and what had been a row of houses could be seen through the gaping wall as a pile of rubble. Where the friends were who had survived four years of occupation I didn't know. The gunfire continued and Mother looked out and saw the beach in front of our house covered by thousands of men firing as they ran up the slope. She said the sea and sand were red, but I could not see how anyone would have enough paint to cause that. Tanks and other vehicles were swarming off the small flat ships onto and up the beach towards our house. Under the table again.

After what seemed like forever, but was probably not even lunchtime, it went quieter, and we heard English voices. We gingerly crept out to see a group of soldiers who seemed surprised to see us. One was smoking and offered Mother a cigarette: another gave me a lump of chocolate. Mother found some Normandy cider that the soldiers gladly drank. Soon they were replaced by even more men, tanks and guns. I had never seen so many men and equipment and it seemed as though the ground would give way.

The next day no one seemed to mind us moving about, but we kept away from burning tanks and all the big equipment and tents where men were being treated. Soldiers lay all over the beach (I hoped that they were all sleeping); buildings that I had seen for years were no more, and it really was a sight that I could not understand. It was days before the sound of gun-fire ceased, and life became as normal as possible with the constant rumble of vehicles through our small town. We missed the electricity, and the toilets didn't work, but that seemed a small price compared with all that we saw around us. An upturned tank lay in what had been our playground. Although the crew were buried elsewhere, we still lay flowers there every 6th of June. An up side was that, because our school was flattened, summer term ended a month early. Even today, 65 years on, every time I pass a memorial or cemetery with its rows of white Portland stone I think about what I saw, and wonder how anyone could have let it happen. Our house was rebuilt in its original design and we again look out over stunning beaches, but memories are not easily erased.

My holiday over, I left Normandy and returned on North Seas Ferries wondering what my memories would have been if the invasion had been on the Northumbria Coast stretching from Bamburgh to the Tyne, and Newcastle and Morpeth had been flattened instead of Caen and St Lo.

Wartime Landmarks

1939	
May/June	Women's Land Army formed, to help food production on farms. Anderson shelters distributed
August/September	Gas-masks distributed
1 September	Germany invaded Poland. Blackout and Child Evacuation started.
3 September	Britain, France, Australia, New Zealand declared war on Germany. Canada declared war on Sept 10. Conscription to Armed Forces introduced for all fit men age 18-41
Mid September	Registration for Identity Cards
November	Ration Books issued (food)
December	Petrol rationing introduced
1940	Food rationing began. First British Restaurants opened. Schoolchildren given vitamins every week. Iron railings removed from parks, walls and gardens
11 March	Meat rationing began
10 May	Germany invaded France. Winston Churchill became Prime Minister. Dig for Victory campaign
14 May	Local Defence Volunteers recruited (renamed in July as the Home Guard). Road signs and milestones removed during May and June
26 May to June	Evacuation of British Expeditionary Force from Dunkirk
10 June	Italy declared war on Britain and France

30 June	Germany occupied Channel Islands
July to September	Battle of Britain: RAF repelled German bombers, helped by radar
1941	
May	Utility clothing introduced
June	Clothing rationing began
22 June	Germany invaded Russia
December	Food points introduced. Single women (20-30) called to war jobs
7 December	Pearl Harbor bombed, and soon after America joined the Allies
14 December	Japan invaded Philippines, Burma, Hong Kong
1942	First American GIs in England
	Mass murders began at Auschwitz
February	Singapore fell to Japanese
June	German General Rommel captured Tobruk (North Africa)
1943	One in ten of 18-25 year old conscripts ('Bevin Boys') were directed to work in coal mines as their National Service
Mid May	Allied victories in North Africa
Late May	Germans and Italians withdrew from North Africa
	Germans withdrew their Atlantic fleet of submarines and ships
10 July	Allies invaded Italy
	Germans defeated at Stalingrad. Russian, British and Indian troops entered Burma
3 September	Italy signed armistice, but Fascists still resisted
13 October	Italy declared war on Germany

1944	
6 June	D-Day. Allies landed at four beaches in Normandy
25 August	Allies liberated Paris
1945	Germany blasted London with V1 and V2 rockets
21 April	Russians reached Berlin, followed by British and Americans
28 April	Italian Fascist leader, Mussolini, executed by partisans
30 April	German leader, Hitler, committed suicide
8 May	VE Day (Victory in Europe)
6 and 9 August	America dropped two atom bombs on Japan
11 August	Japan surrendered. VJ Day declared (Victory over Japan) on 15th
7-16 September	Last Japanese forces surrendered in China, Burma, Hong Kong
1946	New Look in fashion, with longer, full skirts, introduced in Paris. Peacetime National Service (18 months) for all 18 year old fit men
1948	Bevin Boys service ended
1950 21 October	Women's Land Army disbanded
1952	Identity Cards ended
1954	Rationing in Britain ended
1963	Last National Serviceman demobbed

Food ration books were used from 8 January 1940

Weekly allowances per person in 1941 were:
Cheese: 2oz [56g]   Margarine: 4oz [113g] Butter: 2oz [56g] Tea: 2oz [56g] Sugar: 8oz [227g]   Bacon and ham: 4oz [113g]   Eggs: one   Milk: 2 or 3 pints

Per month: *Sweets (from 1942): 12oz [340g]* **Per two months:** *Jam: 1lb [453g]*

You had to register with one shop, which was allocated supplies by number of customers. The shopkeeper cut the week's unperforated tokens out of the ration book (later they were stamped). A points scheme started in December 1941. Sixteen points, which could be used at any shop, were allocated for each month. They were for such items as tinned meat, tinned fruit, condensed milk and breakfast cereal, when available. From March 1940 fresh meat was also rationed to 6oz [170g] a week. Spam (tinned processed meat) and offal were generally available. For the most part bread (usually wholemeal) and vegetables were not rationed. In many cities, canteen-like British Restaurants were set up, primarily for office and industrial workers but open to the general public. A three-course hot meal and cup of tea could be bought for a shilling [5p] without requiring coupons.

Clothing coupons from June 1941

The 66 points a year were considered to be enough for one complete outfit of clothing, including underwear and shoes. Conformity to utility regulations was made compulsory in 1942. Women's skirts had to end no lower than the knee. Men's trousers had no turn-ups and no more than two pockets, with no more than three buttons on jackets. Government advice was offered on eg turning two dishcloths into a jumper, a pillowcase into a blouse, or a worn tweed overcoat into a skirt and jacket. Old silk parachutes could sometimes be bought without coupons for making into underwear or blouses.

Swords into ploughshares: blockhouse into stable at Blyth, Northumberland

Additional Reading

Armstrong, Craig (2007) *Tyneside in the Second World War.* Chichester: Phillimore & Co.

Buckton, Henry (2009) *The Children's Front: The Impact of the Second World War on British Children* Chichester: Phillimore & Co.

Green, Ben (1994) *Britain at War.* Godalming: Colour Library Books.

Gone but not Forgotten: Newcastle at War (1985) City of Newcastle upon Tyne: Newcastle City Libraries

Langford, Liesbeth (2009) *Written by Candlelight.* Hexham: Ergo Press

Acknowledgements for illustrations

Illustrated Magazine, 30 August 1941 (Uncle Robert with Churchill and Roosevelt)
US Air Force Historical Research Agency (Liberator bomber)
www.clydesite.co.uk (ss Gloucester Castle)
www.military-aircraft.org.uk (Hurricane fighter)
www.cyber-heritage.co.uk (AA gun)
www.woodlands-junior.kent.sch.uk (building Anderson shelters)
www.archives.gov (poster)
www.macksites.com/images (barrage balloon)
http://en.wikipedia.org (Handley Page HP42)
www.diggerhistory.info/pages-air-support (Wellington bomber)
www.commons.wikimedia.org (HMS The Prince of Wales)
www.navalhistory.net (HMS St Brides Bay)
www.fleetairarmarchive.net (HMS Victorious)
Alec Bamford
Ruth Lesser
Sylvia Warren
Robert Weiner

We believe the illustrations we have sourced from websites are all in the public domain, but if we have unintentionally infringed copyright please contact newcastleu3a@hotmail.com

The authors

The authors of this book are members of British U3As (Universities of the Third Age). These are not-for-profit educational co-operatives of older people who, through sharing their knowledge, skills and experience, learn from each other. Since 1981 it has been one of the most successful exercises in social co-operation, radical adult education and older generation citizenship in Britain. Anyone retired can join. No qualifications are required and none are given. There are no exams. Learning is for pleasure and membership fees are minimal. The autonomous U3As together form the only national educational organisation in the UK run entirely by its own (250,000) members.

The hundreds of U3As throughout the world have a growing membership pursuing an extensive range of topics - some academic, others recreational. U3As offer opportunities to study, socialise, foster a fitter mind and body and be creative. The production of this book is an example.

Newcastle U3A, Unit 3, 1 Pink Lane, Newcastle upon Tyne, NE1 5DW, UK Tel:(44)(0) 191 230 4430
newcastleu3a@hotmail.com   www.nru3a.co.uk
Registered UK Charity No 1078961

CPSIA information can be obtained at www.ICGtesting.com
Printed in the USA
LVOW081927100812

293859LV00020B/75/P